EXPLORING THE THRESHOLD

07113

3|8|15

19/69

~~Dea~~
Dov.

WITHDRAWN

Please return on or before the latest date above.
You can renew online at *www.kent.gov.uk/libs*
or by telephone 08458 247 200

LP

133.9102

CUSTOMER SERVICE EXCELLENCE

Libraries & Archives

00884\DTP\RN\07.07   LIB 7

EXPLORING THE THRESHOLD

Life As a Medium

Dilys Gater

CHIVERS

British Library Cataloguing in Publication Data available

This Large Print edition published by AudioGO Ltd, Bath, 2013.
Published by arrangement with the Author

U.K.   Hardcover   ISBN   978 1 4713 3971 4
U.K.   Softcover   ISBN   978 1 4713 3972 1

Printed and bound in Great Britain by
MPG Books Group Limited

CONTENTS

Foreword by David Bradbury

Introduction

Part One: A Liminal Realm
'Walking from one life into another, the pilgrim inhabits a liminal realm…'

The Pupil—Teachings of my Spirit Guide
1 Setting Out
      The Tarot—A Book of Reference
2 The Fool
3 The Initiate
      To the Threshold—My journey begins
      The Wise Woman's Path
      The Shrine of Sirona

4 The Novice Medium—Interview
1 Basics of Mediumship
List of Definitions

Part Two: Death & the Maiden
'You walk in moonlight, in the half-light, on the enchanted strand…'

My mediumship begins

v

The Wheel Turns

vii

Author's Notes

I am greatly indebted to the various authors from whose work I have quoted. If full details are not given here, more information on the authors and their books can be obtained on the Internet.

I would especially like to acknowledge my debt to Michael Flatley's Lord of the Dance *(Sidgwick & Jackson, 2006).*

I have for convenience referred to the medium, the artist and so on largely as 'he' throughout—for in spirit as in art, there are no 'isms' except in the minds of beholders.

The interviews offer basic information that hopefully will be helpful to the novice psychic or medium as well as of interest to the general reader. They are of course largely based on my own experience and my accounts may differ from those of other mediums. I have tried to include factual information often lacking in books by workers in this field, as most psychics and mediums (and artists) are intuitive—the old word 'sensitive' sums this up well—and find it difficult to articulate how they work.

The book presents my own thoughts and views as a working medium. I have no wish to be dogmatically confrontational about any beliefs of others.

'Swinging away from dogma, we lost all grip upon spirituality, confusing two things which have little connection with each other—indeed my experience is that the less the dogma the greater the spirituality.'
Arthur Conan Doyle
The Romance of Medicine

'The most beautiful thing we can experience is the mysterious.
It is the source of all true art and science.'
Albert Einstein

'Your talent is God's gift to you—
what you do with it is your gift back to God.'
Television series ER

Foreword
by
David Bradbury

I've known Dilys for the best part of a decade through her association with The Regent Theatre and Victoria Hall in Stoke-on-Trent. She has consistently been a staunch supporter of the arts in Staffordshire, and has played a crucial part in broadening interest and widening participation in the cultural life of the region.

Her unique approach to life is enlightening and her work on the subject of mediumship has, from the very beginning, supplemented and developed my own interest in that area. This book follows in that tradition, and will I'm sure, develop and complement the interests of many budding mediums.

David Bradbury is Group Press Officer for the Ambassador Theatre Group

Dedications

To my husband Paul Gater—
without whose practical help and support
this book could never have been written.
Thanks for helping me survive in the
'real world'.

To David Owen Norris—
international man of music and letters
in respectful appreciation of his enthusiasm and
inspiration
and grateful thanks for his friendship and
generosity.

To Ellen Kent—
for the integrity of her theatrical vision
with thanks and love.

*

Thanks to Ray Johnson for his support,
To Jaine and Helen,
To DHS
To Richard.
And in loving memory of Glo, Fat-face & Mr G.

INTRODUCTION

'How did I get here?'—'It was ordained'
'What must I do?'—'Be there and be your self'

'Shine and be... You have to say yes to
everything, not just a part.
And shine with your whole heart.'

The Pupil
Conversations with Mist

'The average person...knows neither himself nor
his destiny
and he gropes about in life like a child in the
dark'

Elisabeth Haich
(Translated by D Q Stephenson)
The Wisdom of the Tarot

I have been a professional author and novelist
all my working life; Arts and Theatre Editor of
several glossy magazines—and now on-line—
for over a decade. My world involves books
and journalism, printing, publishing, writing
features on all forms of theatre. But I have
also practised as a psychic medium for some
twenty years, counselling the public and
producing books about my spiritual work

1

and development. In fact all these are inter-related—but what do they have in common?

A medium is someone who stands between the 'real world' as most people know it and the unseen, unachievable yet perceived realm or realms that may exist beyond the evidence of our human senses. A spiritual medium trains his mind and body for use as a channel between the world of the living and those of entities existing in spirit or some other form, passing on whatever communications might emerge; but there are many other equally dedicated mediums who do the same, though they may be called by different names.

You do not have to be a 'religious' or even professed 'spiritual' person to be a medium. You may not be 'good' or even very likeable; you can be difficult, opinionated, eccentric, passionately and selfishly driven. Anyone who dedicates their life to any kind of discipline that allows them access to wisdom and truth, in whatever form, is acting as a medium—in the sense of the word meaning a channel, a way, a conduit—for communication with dimensions beyond this one.

All creative artists are mediums. Composer, musician, painter, dancer, writer—each in his way must subject himself to rigorous discipline, whether mental, physical or both, in order to let the interpretive power of 'inspiration' or 'art' or whatever other term is used, pass through and emerge as something relevant and valuable to humanity.

It is easy enough to chronicle the lives of recognised artists of greatness. The pianist who must practise hours at a time, the ballet student whose daily *barre* comes before everything else, the writer who is willing to suffer persecution rather than abandon his vision of the truth. They are perceived as obviously busy *doing* something—something the average person cannot do himself. But beyond the strict physical discipline which is where the artist begins, there is a mindset that also has to be cultivated. However technically brilliant, the artist will never achieve greatness unless his whole consciousness is open to that something greater than himself which can lift his performance onto another plane and catch a glimpse, however fleeting, of some further, mysterious but wonderful dimension of being. Beyond the evidence of our physical senses, great art speaks to us in language we do not understand but which touches our souls.

'There are truths of a subtle, synthetic and divine order, to express which in all their inviolate completeness, human language is incapable. Only music can sometimes make the soul feel them, only ecstasy can show them in absolute vision…'

Au Seuil du Mystere

This point marks the mysterious and

wonderful threshold eventually achieved by the medium. It takes a journey of many years where he struggles to go forward, acknowledging each difficult step. You realize you have reached a place which is beyond the physical, yet still with physical boundaries. You have left the world and yet are a part of it; you have awareness of other worlds but are not there either. You stand between. Your life at this point becomes an exploration of the threshold on which you stand—your daily purpose to discover how best to exist there, how to bring others to an awareness of it. However perceived, artists of all kinds have been aware of and tried to express this concept.

- Igor Stravinsky, the Russian composer who was one of the most influential figures in 20th century music, composed his seminal work *The Rite of Spring (Le Sacre du Printemps)* in an intense effort of concentration which drained him to the point of physical collapse. Living in one tiny room, working through the days and sleeping heavily through the nights, he said later: *'I heard and I wrote what I heard. I was the vessel through which the Sacre passed.'*
- In a different musical sphere composer Brian Wilson, the troubled genius of the Beach Boys, described his music this way: *'It brings spiritual love, unconditional*

spiritual love'.

- The poet John Masefield wrote to a young ballet dancer who had told him of 'the exaltation which a dancer sometimes feels in attaining a momentary perfection': *'Perhaps all the artists share that exaltation, which may be due to the fact that in their different perfections they touch the Universal rhythm, which keeps the stars in their courses and the planets in their dance.'*
- The dancer Isadora Duncan wrote: *'Now I am going to reveal to you something which is very pure, a totally white thought...The dance is love, it is only love, it alone and that is enough...'*
- *'When you listen to Bach you hear a part of God...When you watch me dance you see a part of God',* declared Rudolf Nureyev.

It is difficult to find words when speaking of the act of mediumship. Most mediums—especially the artist whose expression of his art is physical—fall back as we see here, on vague terms like 'love' or even 'God'. Psychic mediums talk about consciously 'working with Spirit'.

What then is the nature of this term, being or thing called 'Spirit'? Words like 'Spirit', 'Light', 'Source'—even 'God'—actually convey very little and efforts to define them achieve even less since they are so subjective. That is why throughout history the unexplained

5

secrets of the spiritual and the divine and all communications with them have been referred to as just that—The Mysteries.

My work as a medium is not 'religious'. It does not advocate any particular belief, discipline or dogma, for I am consulted by people of every faith. Neither do I claim to provide proof—of eternal life, life beyond the grave, survival of the soul or anything else. There was never a truer saying than that:

'For those who believe, no proof is necessary
For those who do not believe, no proof will convince'—

I take it for granted that any reader who opens this book will already be aware that there are other dimensions beyond our own and will not want to waste time speculating about existence after death or whether souls survive. Hopefully they are more interested in hearing what it is like to communicate with the inhabitants of further dimensions as I do on a regular basis, what we might be able to offer each other, details of the why and the how of a life dedicated to mediumship.

'I feel more and more every day, as my
imagination strengthens,
that I do not live in this world alone, but in a
thousand worlds.'

John Keats

PART ONE
A LIMINAL REALM

*'Walking from one life into another, the pilgrim
inhabits a liminal realm...'*
Frances Wilson
The Ballad of Dorothy Wordsworth

'limen...liminal' (Latin—threshold)
Mini Oxford Dictionary

*'The soul's dark cottage, battered and decayed
Lets in new light through chinks that time has
made;
Stronger by weakness, wiser men become,
As they draw near to their eternal home.
Leaving the old, both worlds at once they view,
That stand upon the threshold of the new.'*

Edmund Waller
Of the Last Verses in the Book

The Pupil
Teachings of my Spirit Guide

Many of the references in this book are taken from communications I have held over the years with my spiritual guide Mist. The only true reference any medium ever has are the personal sources of wisdom with which he connects and works—his 'Spirit Guides'—for mediumship is a hands-on profession, you learn from your own unfolding experience rather than that of others. Often venturing into unfamiliar territory, you have to be able to trust your guides implicitly: like rock-climbers or explorers of inhospitable terrain, but also on a deeper spiritual level, you need to put yourself—your life, sanity and soul—into the hands of your guides and it is vital that you know they will not fail you.

As a conscientious writer, I have kept a record of all my communications with Mist. The early ones largely reflected my agonizing and on-going self-doubt, hesitancy and questioning from day to day, week to week as I struggled to follow the path to which I had been called. Over time, however, as with most mediums, the 'conversations' went on to chronicle the growth of an intimate relationship of trust and dependence on both sides. I will be discussing the nature of spiritual guidance in more detail later, but Mist's words of wisdom and truth quoted here illustrate how, as I progressed in awareness, I continued to regard myself very much as 'The Pupil' in the presence of a highly elevated Master.

'Are you my guardian angel or spirit guide?
Are there such things as spirit guides?'

'I am here to teach you, for you asked (for me).
I was always there but far off.'

The Pupil
Conversations with Mist

1
SETTING OUT

'Truth is a pathless land, and you cannot
approach it by any path whatsoever, by any
religion, by any sect.'

Jiddu Krishnamurti

Life as a psychic medium started off for
me having a great deal in common with the
entertainment business.

'The lifestyle I was now following was
entirely different from any life I had previously
known,' I recalled in *The Urban Shaman*. 'It
involved travelling several times a week and
most weekends for long distances to attend
Psychic Fairs and events in dozens of different
venues that ranged from elegant ballrooms,
Town Halls, five star hotels, the barns of
country hostelries to Community, Health
or Healing Centres (in one case, directly
overlooking a busy swimming pool) and tacky
rooms at the back of run-down London pubs.
I actually loved every moment and quickly
learned the rules—that a psychic, like the
actress I had always longed to be if I had not
been a writer, was always in the spotlight,
always on duty; that it was important to be
there, not to let the public down; that however

ill one felt one never missed a 'performance' but somehow struggled to make it, to be ready in costume and make-up for when the doors opened, when the 'curtain rose'.

'I travelled to give consultations in private houses (from council semis to unbelievable mansions, one belonging to a Bollywood star) and saw sitters at home. I worked both as a psychic and a trader in Portobello Road and many of the other London markets. I carried out readings and gave healing in the most incongruous of settings that ranged from a converted railway carriage in Camden Market to 'car boots' in windy meadows, pouring rain or sub-zero temperatures; from 'stately homes' to marquees and tents, wine bars and coffee-shops, fashion and jewellery emporiums to a casino. I gave demonstrations and interviews in radio and TV studios and on location, from filming in a candle-lit church to midnight 'phone-ins' sitting in my flat in my dressing gown and slippers.'

Spiritual mediums are difficult to categorize. You can go from the extremes of earnest individuals who rarely smile and present themselves with images of praying hands, stained-glass windows and vases of funeral lilies, to what I once described as:

'... *a weird eccentric clanking amulets, sitting in a darkened room holding one-sided*

12

conversations with an unseen but exotically named 'Spirit Guide' (often sounding like a comedy performer who missed his vocation on the stage) while other spirits that might be present are spookily requested to participate by knocking on the table—'Twice for yes, once for no!"

But is one born a medium? How does one know this is one's fated path, where and how to get going? The medium James Byrne wrote in *The Psychic World of James Byrne*: *'It is totally impossible to teach anyone to be a medium. God decides who will be gifted in that way, and all the instruction on earth can never produce that gift. However, having the gift and developing it, to the point where it can function for the benefit of mankind, are separate matters.'*

Some people—like me—come to mediumship in mid-life though the gift might have been there unacknowledged from the beginning. One prominent trance medium I met at the College of Psychic Studies, for instance, revealed that she had previously followed a successful career in the fashion industry. Others may perceive and accept early on in their lives that this is their lifetime's work—a personal calling, a conscious choice, an acceptance of vocation, a philosophy of learning. The medium Stephen O'Brien recalled in his book *Voices from Heaven*:

'I've had these psychic abilities from my earliest years, visions of other worlds beyond death often coming to me in the strangest

13

ways, and at the oddest moments…As a baby, just a few months old, I can vividly recall strange faces peering at me over my cot-gate at night…'

But however or wherever you start, the medium's road is a long one, often barely recognized. It continues to evolve for you never suddenly 'become a medium' and that is that. It would imply that you stopped progressing, whereas new facets are constantly being revealed, new choices continuously becoming apparent: there is always more to learn.

Whatever kind of medium you may be—artist, musician, writer, dancer as well as spiritual traveller—you are likely to live a life very different to the recognized 'norm'. You must place yourself at the disposal of your inspiration, your art (however you perceive your driving force) as a power you recognize as greater than yourself. Your life is spent in this service and is not your own: but this is a willing sacrifice. However difficult, tormented or tortuous the way, the rewards are compensatingly sublime.

No artist or medium ever seriously wants to lose his gift, to be 'ordinary'. He lives with normally accepted barriers to intuitive vision removed, he explores dimensions and worlds unknown and unseen by the great majority of people, he has access to an existence that transcends human living. Though his visions may only be glimpsed in brief snatches, even these are worth it.

While creative artists are generally tolerated within the community even if their behaviour is regarded as 'peculiar', 'odd', 'driven by the muse', a psychic medium is likely to find himself set inescapably apart from the norm. He discovers and has to acknowledge publicly that he is connecting with—working with—a separate entity usually referred to as we have seen, as Spirit—the capital letter in recognition that this is a name or title not just a generalization.

It can be difficult for others to accept that you live in close proximity to an actual Higher Being or Power with which you regularly communicate, and though the medium spends much of his time struggling for obedience and humility, the fact that he appears to be claiming some sort of personal 'hot-line to the Divine' sounds like the exact opposite. People do not understand that mediumship has nothing to do with 'religion' as such—or else they go to the other extreme and assume a medium has no belief in any 'God' at all. But a large percentage of gifted workers in this field are likely to have passed through a serious crisis of faith and actually 'lost their religion' at some time or another—maybe more than once. Often it is necessary for all previous indoctrination of a 'religious' nature to be rejected as inadequate before the medium is able to begin following his destined path, being taught how to work for and with Spirit by Spirit itself, in whatever form the teaching is presented.

It was not until I was in my forties that I became aware of my gifts, recognized the call of Spirit and was able to accept what I was being asked to do. But being a writer first, a medium second gave me valuable insight into both vocations—their similarities as well as their differences. Vocational artists often suffer very much as they try to express their art and may damage themselves mentally and physically in their efforts to follow where their inspiration takes them. It can be equally agonizing for the novice medium, but in spite of what is sometimes said about the difficulty of 'carrying the burden' of artistic genius or spiritual insight with its painful awareness and responsibility, I have found the gift of mediumship is never forced. At every turn Spirit gives you a choice and you are free to refuse if you want to.

In my experience few people refuse, even though they might not be able to live up to their good intentions. Once knowing what it is like to work with Spirit, the prospect of living without it is bleak in the extreme. The closer you grow to Spirit, the more unthinkable becomes the alternative and someone like myself, doing the work I do, lives and exists in increasingly closer proximity to the world of Spirit than to the world of 'real life'.

To a casual observer, life as a medium might sound pretty grim. You do not consider what 'I' might do or want. You abandon control, follow guidelines that very often are not clear. You never ask 'why?' You do not need to ask questions for you will be given any answers you need. Once the call comes you realize you have been highly blessed and never, however difficult the way, want to turn back. More and more, you become aware that working with Spirit means a complete surrender of self, that as a servant of Spirit you must devote your life to doing what you are told. Yet in this amazing two-way process you are rewarded with riches that are not of this world, given food for your soul, inner sustenance and comfort on the long journey through human living; you experience a sense of kinship and companionship with wise and elevated guides and teachers.

Though we appear to progress chronologically, learning as we go, one of the most notable features about working with Spirit is that there is never any 'beginning' to the consciousness of truth, no progression in learning wisdom as we imagine it. The ability

17

to relate to truth—on whatever level this is achieved at any given time—is purely a state of mind. And anyone trying to follow a similar path will find himself travelling in circles, in spirals, through labyrinths, into the mirror-images of his own reflections, even backwards, vertically or in other directions difficult to describe as awareness and consciousness expands.

The novice discovers surges and plateaus of energy and revelation; becomes enabled to live by other measures than those of time and place; learns to explore parallel universes and become familiar with different aspects of his true self and true reality. Spirit does not bring itself down to our level when communicating: we grow instead to understand and appreciate the complexities of whatever has been communicated as we ourselves become more elevated, more able to learn. This is one way teachings of any kind can be tested. If they continue to grow with the pupil, so even the master finds new instruction and wisdom within them day by day then they are valid, otherwise they have no genuine worth.

The daily journey is lived in spiritual intensity and on other planes of existence; the more experienced one becomes, the more one withdraws into a whole different attitude to this world and other people in it. In the beginning the novice medium is likely to feel he is there 'to help others' by passing on such messages of enlightenment and comfort as he receives: continuing to work with Spirit he becomes aware that his first duty is to himself, to progress spiritually so he can meet the challenges, learn the lessons that will enable him to become more spiritually mature.

I started off as most psychics do with the burning conviction that I had a task to perform for Spirit—to help and assist others who might consult me; to reveal the reality of the spiritual world in the way I lived and conducted myself. As I followed my spiritual guides and learned from them I identified myself as time passed as a 'Celtic Wise Woman' (the name of one of my books), there to advise others of the choices they could make, the ways they too could go.

After many years and a great deal of experience, I perceived my role begin to change without any conscious effort—or even desire—on my part. Like the mediaeval monks who spent their lives illuminating old manuscripts to the glory of God, I sensed more and more the need to devote myself to consciously serving Spirit in my daily living, to make a withdrawal from a material existence. The commitment was total and from being simply a traveller, a pilgrim who shared my experiences and thoughts in order to help others, I was aware that I had been given a role serving Spirit on a deeper and more

19

personal level. I had progressed from being a 'Wise Woman', there to serve the community, to service as a votive, a privately avowed priestess of the shrine, actively involved in the Mysteries.

The term 'working with Spirit' can, as with the term 'Spirit' itself, be interpreted in different ways. A psychologist might view evidence of this state of mind as indicative of mental imbalance and many psychics, mediums and artists do in fact exist on a fine line between visionary mysticism, genius and insanity—I have walked that road myself and written books about my experiences. As a writer I also know those states of inspiration in which an intuitive artist produces work he feels has been 'granted' from somewhere or someone outside himself. This is almost impossible for the 'ordinary' person to comprehend and it is a tough path, often endured in painful mental isolation.

It is commonly believed that the sole activity of psychic or spiritual mediums is to spend time morbidly 'talking to the dead'. Most mediums begin at this level because the emotional ties between us and our loved ones make the world of the dead closer and easier to contact; and some mediums do not progress beyond this stage. But more advanced mediumship involves communication with—

and often mental journeys into—other dimensions and worlds, other planes of awareness and interaction with very different kinds of beings. And essentially, this searching, this groping into unknown territories to try and reach the Source is also what creative artists do. All are conduits—ways or channels—for instinctively felt truths and intuitive knowledge.

'There was little recognition in my peer group for the powerful urge I always felt to further my spiritual dimension. In this, I was as much an outcast as the struggling dancer, artist or poet.'

Dr. Donald Schnell (Prema Baba Swamiji)
The Initiation

Am I progressing? I try hard—at least, I think I do—

Do not judge yourself or any other thing. It is not for you to judge. There is no need to try. Simply be to the utmost of which you are capable and the rest will follow.

The Pupil
Conversations with Mist

21

The Tarot
A Book of Reference

It is generally believed that mediums deal directly with Spirit and do not use crystals, tarot cards, runes or any other divinatory tool. Many do not. But I started my psychic career as a psychic rather than a medium and during the course of years working regularly in Psychic Fairs, had the opportunity to sample nearly every system of working there is. I found the tarot pack of cards, which I have studied for nearly twenty years, offers consistently enlightening comment on all matters, whether of this world or worlds beyond.

So as a practising psychic medium I use the tarot as a tool to focus the intuitive vision in the same way a joiner might use a hammer or an electrician a screw-driver. The tarot has many ways of giving advice and guidance— essentially practical, it is filled with basic common-sense; it explores the journey of the soul with advanced insight into the world of spirit but is non-religious, though its truths can be found in the teachings of most formal religions; on every level, in every mood, at every crisis, during times of joy as well as lighting the way through dark days, the tarot is perpetually new yet always the same.

The concepts it embodies reflect innumerable sources of ancient wisdom including that of the Celts, the 'wise men' of the east, the magi of ancient Mesopotamia and Egypt; the shamans of ancient Siberia and the north; and all places and races where civilization began and has flourished and continued to grow.

'It seems likely that the Tarot cards and in particular the Major Arcana were devised to represent grades or stages in a system of initiation. It is possible to interpret the meanings of the cards in terms of a sequence of events or lessons to be learned. There seem to be close links with the system of alchemy whose devotees believed in the 'Hermetic' philosophy and underwent training leading to spiritual enlightenment.'

Bill Anderton
Tarot

2
THE FOOL

Everyone else thinks I'm a fool—

Fool card my darling child.
(Referring to the Fool card in the Tarot pack)

So that is what it really means. No wonder,
but I didn't think the Fool actually *felt* foolish.
The Pupil
Conversations with Mist

'Remember that the fool in the eyes of the gods
and the fool in the eyes of man are very
different.'
Oscar Wilde
De Profundis

Mediumship as public entertainment is
actually nothing new—mediums now appear
in their own TV shows and go on performance
tours, but the wheel has simply turned full
circle since the early part of the 20th century.
Devotees of stories by Agatha Christie and
other writers of the period will be familiar
with society hostesses who regularly call on
'Madame X', the medium, to hold séances to
entertain their guests. Agatha Christie was
very interested in—and respectful of—psychic

matters and wrote many stories of interest to students of the occult; Noel Coward's creation of the scatty Madame Arcati in his play *Blithe Spirit*, was based on his observation of working mediums.

Mediumship was regarded originally as the province of adults and not suitable for children but the late 20th century saw a remarkable shift of attitude in that anything to do with the occult was down-graded to the status of amusement for the young. Wizardry in the form of the Arthurian Merlin or the trainee Harry Potter has taken its place alongside Vampires and Vampire Slayers, Teenage Witches, Avatars and similar iconic figures in books and films and on children's TV. Even work like Tolkein's *Lord of the Rings* is prone to being casually dismissed by the public as within the same category rather than recognized for what it is—a serious comment on the nature of Good and Evil.

This is a highly significant move, since as far back as the reign of Henry VIII, any kind of meddling with the occult has been considered dangerous in the extreme. Henry's Witchcraft Act of 1542 was the first to declare witchcraft (which the public perception still confuses with mediumship) a felony punishable by death; later Acts increased the severity of the punishment to include confiscation of the property and assets not only of those found guilty but of any who consulted them: this purely financial motive, apart from spiritual fervour, was what prompted many so-called 'witch hunters' to pursue their activities with such zeal.

1950 was the last year when a medium was threatened with the Witchcraft Act of 1735, though celebrated cases had continued through the early part of the 20th century, most notoriously involving the medium Helen Duncan, who in 1944 went to prison for nine months. It seemed a step forward when in 1951 the Witchcraft Act was replaced by the Fraudulent Mediums Act at the instigation of Spiritualists—but there was a sting in the tail. Largely, the official stance seemed to be that anyone claiming to be 'a psychic, medium or other spiritualist' was probably conning the public and was therefore liable to prosecution. The inference was that money was changing hands, for people quietly carrying out their mediumship privately or with friends could hardly be accused of conning anyone; mediums serving Spiritualist churches—who traditionally receive only their expenses—were also presumably exempt. Officialdom has an extremely ambivalent attitude towards occult activity; it avoids the whole subject of any 'genuine' mediumship and concerns itself only with exposing possible fraud.

When the Fraudulent Mediums Act of 1951 was repealed in 2008, we might have assumed that 'genuine' psychics, mediums,

26

and spiritualists would have been free to practise and if necessary earn their livings with a public appreciation of the seriousness of their work. Instead, it appears legally necessary to issue a disclaimer that all such work is 'purely for entertainment (sometimes 'experimental') purposes.' Various authorities concerned—TV programmers and theatre managements, for example—all do this. So we must presume there is some hidden agenda of our times which denigrates the nature of Good and Evil, other worlds and dimensions and any suggestion of spiritual power (unless 'approved' by officialdom) as mere triviality, there to provide entertainment for the young and the gullible.

Performances before paying audiences are obviously geared to entertain and have little to do with the development path of individual mediums (or of those who might consult them). 'Madame X' and her kind gave their sitters a glimpse into hidden worlds that provided the same kind of thrill as the lectures of explorers who had ventured into darkest Africa or tried to reach the Pole. Modern performance tours and shows too, give a very stereotypical idea of what mediumship and mediums are all about; the vocational element of spiritual seeking is lost in an attitude of 'mediumship-on-demand', solely there to provide what the public asks for rather than the more difficult instructional truths and

27

challenges Spirit may want to impart.

I personally will not undertake mediumship just because someone requests it; often the seeker's message is to learn to find his own inner strength and wisdom rather than rely on those who have passed on to guide him. Mediumship does not provide any sort of 'quick fix' and Spirit may remain silent, or even confront enquirers with facts they do not want to face. An experienced medium never provides an answer if Spirit has chosen not to give one, or even feels the need to apologize for apparent failure to communicate. Nothing can be guaranteed: the medium's duty should always be to Spirit rather than to any enquirer—and most certainly not to TV viewers or theatre audiences who want to see some action and who, if they do not get it, will demand their money back.

I have always been a maverick—one who will not follow the crowd. In my schooldays I was a noted innovator with ideas that brought me continually to the notice of my tutors; I abandoned possible nine-till-five employment for precarious freelance writing where in the course of researching history and philosophy (among other things) I learned to think for myself, develop my own concepts and form my own conclusions as well as absorb the ideas and opinions of others.

28

An undoubtedly brainy person with a quick mind, I began to pride myself on my ability to investigate and formulate theories beyond the simple, mostly erroneous facts generally accepted as true. Artistically, this resulted in a career where I produced articles and books that were published and read by others; regarding my spiritual development I was equally revolutionary—the one thing I was certain of for years was that I could not trust the stories I had been told about 'religion' (I was brought up a Methodist) though extensive familiarity with the Bible's contents and imagery proved a constant and often unexpectedly useful source of reference.

I 'lost my faith' in my early twenties when I underwent an episode of great trauma and felt there had been no answer to my prayers and God had let me down. I also discovered from my research that much of what was presented as fact in 'religious studies' and in places of worship themselves was highly inaccurate. I read books that confounded all the Biblical texts alongside books that gave various different accounts of well-known historical events and identified these as very similar: history too is written in clichés which are far too ingrained into most people's minds to be changed.

Medium and artist, each must struggle with

his beliefs, rejecting formal instruction in his quest to discover his own completely fresh perspective. Often it is humbling to find after years of rebelling against established teachings or concepts that one has come round in a circle to find a personal version of the very teachings one had previously rejected so violently.

As a young writer I wanted to explode popular myths and reveal new truths—to prove that black might actually have been white, right might have been wrong. I undertook investigative writing of articles and books that explored the truth about popular historical figures and events—the reign of Richard III, for example, the legends of Arthur, the Battle of Hastings, the historical Hamlet, the lives of Anne Boleyn, Mary Queen of Scots and the Brontes. It took many years before I realized that the general public is not seriously bothered about the truth. The average person is quite happy to live with what is comfortable and does not want his realities challenged, even if it can be proved conclusively that those realities are false.

The Fool

The Fool card is the first in the tarot pack, sometimes numbered naught rather than one and occasionally also presented as the last

card, since it marks the completed cycle—
or circle—of the Major Arcana. It usually
shows a young man in rough garb setting off
somewhere with a bundle over his shoulder,
a small dog yapping at his heels. Travelling
light, leaving the trappings of the material
world behind, he is also called 'The Traveller'
or 'The Vagabond': he has abandoned the
accepted road for a perilous track close to a
rocky cliff-edge, though he chooses this route
deliberately.

The Fool is everyone who insists on
following his own star, branching out, doing
his own thing, refusing to be stereotyped in
his search for meaning. So the story of any
medium or artist who 'marches to a different
drum' recounts the same journey, whether
one calls it the shamanic journey or Vision
Quest of indigenous peoples like the Native
American Indians; the sacred journeys of the
ancient Celts whose Druidic training, like that
of shamans, took many years; the adventures
of the mythical knights of Arthurian romance
who set out into the unknown in their search
for the Grail. Such journeys are immense
undertakings that cannot be achieved
overnight. They may take a lifetime and even
then not reach an end, only perhaps an 'end of
the beginning' as Winston Churchill famously
remarked in another context.

Anyone who 'works with Spirit' can expect
to serve an apprenticeship of at least twenty

years before achieving any real maturity in what he does. Life becomes a pilgrimage each individual undertakes in whatever way he must—some memorable names of relatively recent times have illustrated this, whether one chooses to take their beliefs on board or not.

- Edgar Cayce, the 'Sleeping Prophet' dedicated his life to the development of his unique gifts in the furtherance of the work of Spirit and killed himself through exhaustion trying to help too many people at a time of great need during and after the Second World War.

- The founder of Reiki, the discipline of which I am a Master, was Dr. Mikaomi Usui, a Japanese teacher and devout Buddhist. He dedicated his life to developing and teaching the holistic healing art and its philosophy after the Reiki energy was bestowed on him while undergoing a 21-day meditation at Mount Kurama near Kyoto.

- Edward Bach, a Harley Street doctor who later turned to homeopathic medicine, dedicated himself to perfecting his 'Flower Remedies' which work to maintain the natural harmonies of the body. Bach thought illness occurred as the result of 'a contradiction between the purposes of the soul and the personality's point of view.' His flower remedies, which he tested on himself, were based on his belief in the healing energies inherent in the petals of certain flowers and plants, which could be accessed by processing them with water and sunlight.

In the 1950s, Carl Jung wrote in his book later translated as *Flying Saucers: A Modern Myth of Things Seen in the Sky*:

'Untold millions of so called Christians have lost their belief in a real and living mediator, while the believers endeavour to make their belief credible to primitive people, when it would be much more fruitful to bestow these much needed efforts on the white man... it is always so much easier to talk and act down to people instead of up to them...'

His words underline how genuine spiritual pilgrimage (as opposed to alternative New Age lifestyles or the claims of 'divinely inspired' self-help systems to change lives instantly) has over the last half-century become more and more anachronistic in the self-styled sophisticated society that has made the western world an increasingly cynical and shallow place. So what prompts the undertaking of such spiritual journeys, such odysseys? What prompts the novice medium, even? How can one know when and how to begin?

Often scenarios of doom involving 'the end of the world'—some overshadowing our own era—which have persisted throughout history cause individuals to found cults and crusades aspiring to save the world/ the galaxy/ whatever. But before anyone (or anything) else can be saved, it is each individual's responsibility to save himself; and in this sense every sacred journey is a private one, undertaken in faith, not in response to any particular threat to society as a whole but because the time is right for that person.

One of the most enduring inspirational myths in the western world is the Grail Search, which can be interpreted as an intuitive longing for clarity, wisdom and truth: the heroic figures from legend and myth playing a necessary role in inspiring us to higher and better things, encouraging us on in our dreams and destinies. Many people enjoy 'acting out' the idea of following a shamanic or spiritual path in their spare time but most would be seriously scared to commit themselves fully to such a way of life: the spiritual journey is not trivial or 'virtual', nor does it consist of communal fun and games with the like-minded; fluffy clouds and inspirational sunsets, sweetness and light, as many commentators would have us believe.

The shaman's Vision Quest—like the training of the Druidic or other novice in the Mysteries—involves the ultimate in suffering, physical deprivation, possibly even death; the Grail Quest also pledged a lifetime's dedication to a sought but unspecified goal of such complexity and sacredness that in Arthurian legend the knights had only the vaguest vision of what they were really seeking.

The Vision Quest takes the novice into mysterious Other-worlds where he is not sure what is real and what is illusion—and I personally found it was my Celtic background that gave me a recognisable foothold, a place to stand and start from, an identity. Living in close proximity with the natural world, the Celts were consciously aware of the power of nature: to them each lake or stream, each rock or tree had its special spirit or deity. But since this is essentially a journey into the unknown, there are no rules. Whether one accepts the concept of many gods or a single godhead—or even none as such—what the learning process involves is a striving for communication with the Source of Life, the known or unknown Divine; the realisation of wisdom and knowledge through visions, making contact with the intangible in attempting to transcend the material reality of human existence.

You can choose to live with the Divine whether or not you feel you have any recognizable means of access to it. What you experience may be random, intuitive and not come via any known channels—images in the poetry of D H Lawrence as well as William

Blake, for example, express the soul's longing for transcendence, the urgent need to lose oneself in the Light.

Legends intertwine so everyone can find his own inspiration—the Welsh and the Arthurian tales as detailed in the *Mabinogion* meant that I personally felt I might have been walking the same paths trodden by the knights on their Grail Quests as I trod the roads of North Wales. I grew up steeped in such images and visions, though incoherently—even resentfully—for many years. The process of development must have been going on all my life though I was not aware of it.

One passes through an extremely convoluted learning curve trying to find one's way, and the image of the Fool is very appropriate for the novice medium. One may be ridiculed even for making the effort to try, be willing to admit that after all, one might have got it wrong, and have to start all over again; one must honestly own up to one's insecurity and bewilderment, one's personal doubt and fear. The novice who works with Spirit must have the courage to face the unknown with no guarantees of any outcome, favourable or otherwise. Dealings with dimensions other than the physical have to be taken entirely on trust: there is never proof nor certainty as such, whatever circumstantial evidence might be presented.

But there is no certainty in the physical

either, it just seems so because we feel more comfortable with that belief—planning the future confidently, talking about 'next week' and 'next year', though the truth is that next week and next year will never come, we remain constantly in the present. We refer to the past as unarguable historical fact, though our memories of it—like the history books I challenged—may prove just as inaccurate when compared to the recollections of others; even the present can seem very different to different people. The medium must relinquish the comfort zones of time and place, go where he is led, take whatever comes however uncomprehending or ridiculous he feels; he must obey the instructions he is given however stupid or irresponsible his actions might seem to others.

Everything seems to conspire against mediums to make life difficult for them. Their own intellect is an instrument of doubt, their own critical faculty a rational judge that gets in their way. The more aware and able the novice, the more he will be inclined to doubt his personal awareness and ability. Yet what the Fool card teaches us is not to deny our hesitancies and doubts.

As I progressed I realized that doubt is a tool to work with, that certainty—like our concept of security—is in fact the enemy of progress. There is no authoritarian position we can reach where we will have nothing more to learn and can dictate to others. At every stage, we need to see that though we may have made progress, we are not necessarily nearer an end, simply further along the way. We must question all the time, for our doubt and lack of certainty is important. The Fool is wise enough to admit he does not know—and courageous enough to accept that he will often feel foolish.

'The Fool represents ignorance or naivete but shows us that everything we need to begin our spiritual journey and to initiate change is within our grasp... If we place our trust in a higher order we will be guided through the dangers and darkness and into the light. We need only open our eyes and go forward with both awe and courage. As we gain knowledge we will be transformed.'
Rosemary Ellen Guiley and Robert M Place
The Alchemical Tarot

'Mediums must work at their calling with a holy dedication.'
Will Ford, medium and minister of the SNU (Spiritualists National Union)

3
THE INITIATE

'When the Celtic Imagination searched for the structures of shelter and meaning, it raised its eyes to the mountains and the heavens and put its trust in the faithful patterns of the sun, stars, moon and seasons.'

John O'Donohue
Divine Beauty

'The sight of the water in the well as clear as glass, greenish like beryl or aquamarine, trembling at the surface with the force of the springs... quite drew and held my eyes to it... even now the stress and buoyancy and abundance of the water is before my eyes.'

Gerard Manley Hopkins
(on the healing shrine at Holywell, North Wales)

To the Threshold—my journey begins

The Principality of Wales lies westwards to the sea, from the Dee Estuary in the north to the Bristol Channel in the south. To the east is the mound of the earthworks built by King Offa of Mercia to keep the marauding Welsh out of his dominions in the 8th century. Yet there is a shadowy Wales long gone but still there, the ancient Celtic world of mystery and enchantment where the starry landscape of the heavens and abysses of the underworld were as real as the physical landscape of hills and lakes, trees, rocks and thundering seastrand.

The pagan Celts walked with their many deities and saw meaning and wisdom in everyday things—the running of their horses, the turning of a leaf; they heard music in falling water and the call of birds over winter snow. Their shrines were sacred places where pilgrims could seek answers and learn wisdom.

I always knew this land existed. I walked it in delight and in terror while I was growing up, a country child in a North Wales village with no history to speak of, built to house workers at the nearby Steel Works during the mid-1800s. But mine was not your ordinary kind of village. Dragons crouched as dark shapes of mountains against the western skyline and on our very doorstep, fretting on its leash, a huge, encroaching black monster, fire-breathing and threatening, swallowed up the little houses and the roads stealthily by night. The mountain of the Steel Works slag bank, a hundred metres high to a child's eyes, rippled its muscles beneath its scaly skin and inched forward when the waste and clinker from the furnaces was tipped down it. Half of the village—shops, chapels and streets—already lay beneath the Bank.

Our village stood on a spot previously so lonely it was rumoured that the fairies danced there, and some hundred years after being conjured from its grassy glade its end came in the early 1970s in just as drastic a fashion. As part of the Steel Works' programme of expansion, the then owners bought up every house, shop, shed, building and open space and demolished the whole area, razing it to the ground for car parking and open-cast mining— all too soon abandoned when the Works closed some years later. The area returned to wild undergrowth, former roads obliterated, leading nowhere, with ivy thickening round the trees and bushes that grew again to block the way. Like the green valleys drowned in the depths of reservoirs, the ghost of my village now thrums eerily to itself behind the façade of reality: even we cannot tell which is real, which is the memory.

The land is like this. It does not give itself easily. Walk the hills of today and the past

41

will remain closed to you. Visit places whose names roll like glorious poetry from the tongue and you can come away more of a stranger than ever. Yet there is still powerful magic to be found among the scratched ancient maps of kingdoms, princedoms and tribal territories long gone; glimpsed for an instant in the movement of cloud shadows over lake and mountain; sensed where stones sunk in the earth mark the places of meeting and parting, of bloody battle and treacherous betrayal; of the living and loving, the griefs, prayers, hates, yearning and aspiration of the people who have lived here.

During my early years working and studying as a psychic, I spent long hours in the shamanic tradition of mental journeying, seeking my true identity, my true role. I knew I was Welsh and that everyone of Welsh descent could claim to be—in some way—descended from princes, but was that relevant to my spiritual growth?

My lineage and birth was to shape my future. Writing *Celtic Wise Woman* I took as my inspiration some lines passed on to me by a friend. I wove my book round them, wanting to believe them, trusting their inspiration to guide me. Amelia Summerfield was a Reiki Master who gave me my first experience of the gentle, yet immensely powerful Reiki

42

discipline of healing. After that first session she described how she saw me in this image from a past existence:

'Winter and thick snow
out in the Wilderness,
You are a Wise Woman, and you are kneeling down
picking berries,
You've got a staff, you're wearing purple,
Your hair hangs below your waist.'

A further vision came during a forty-two day intensive 'retreat' after I had written *Celtic Wise Woman* when I was going through a particularly difficult patch in my life. I described it in another book as 'a past life recollection of a time and place where I had been and known my true self, reassuring and reaffirming'.

'I experienced a moment of great joy, an instant when I had lived as a true 'Celtic wise woman'—recognised in the community and revered by her people—at some place without a name in 1st or 2nd Century Britain during the time of the Roman occupation. I was standing in deep snow beside an expanse of water, with trees all around. Everything was covered with snow but the sky was intensely blue, the sun was out, the winter day charged with gold. I was wrapped in a thick fur cloak, exhilarated and laughing. Ahead of me, across the icy black water of the

43

lake a dark dot moved, leaving ripples arrowing in straight lines behind it—I knew it for the head of an otter.'

The Wise Woman's Path

'And they saw a tall tree by the side of the river, one half of which was in flames from the root to the top, and the other half was green and in full leaf.'

Matthew Arnold
*On the Study of Celtic Literature
(The Mabinogion)*

Though I grew up in the physical landscape of Wales, like others before me I also walked in landscapes filled with visions. In modern times traditions generally accepted as Celtic are largely Irish, but the tribes of Wales created their own distinctive mythology, music and poetry—and their own magic.

Magic is a focusing of the will and intent, but there is always a price to pay and a responsibility that comes with the power— it is not to be trifled with. Like the alchemist who works with base metals, transmuting them into gold—a metaphor for the transformation of the individual or thing into its purest essence—I had no choice as I grew but to use whatever experience, good or bad, came my way, absorbing it into my blood and bone to work how it would within me.

The 'land of my fathers'—the *'hen wlad fy nhadau'*—of sentimental anthem is a real place, but the words actually translate more as 'the ancient country of fighting men'. Like the 'weekend shamans' I described in *The Urban Shaman*, casual dabblers in ancient Welsh mysticism may find themselves unexpectedly confronted with visions terrifying and hostile, for the Celts were a ruthless people who had swept through the known world, sacking and harrying every civilised community from Rome to Gaul. In Britain they were driven ever westwards until they could go no further. They found themselves in a difficult terrain of mountain, lake and river valley where there were few accessible paths and no comfortable sites to fortify. Here these war-like races found their spiritual home, blending their essence and the best of themselves into the rugged landscape, creating even in peace, the anticipatory expectation of struggle and yet more fighting.

The 'Cymri' as they called themselves—meaning 'the Brotherhood'—have always lived in close proximity to the land and respected its deeply spiritual inspirational qualities as well as its bounty and power. The dynamic of this land is what creates and endows its enduring magic, for though one of the most beautiful countries on earth its history is a

45

story of invasion and defence against invasion. Continuously at war—if not with others then with themselves—the people embody a vision of life's journey as a path of continual discovery and development.

An ancient kingdom wise in suffering, its wisdom remains ever young; its history is drenched in the slaughter of battle, but such sacrificial blood-letting has intuitively invoked the gods rather than sought to propitiate them. All who would learn from this land grow in stature, diminished only by becoming soft or complacent, by any refusal to push their resources to the limit, to continue the long upward climb. Achingly beautiful, bestowing unbearably tender blessings on those who accept and love it unreservedly, this is a land for those who would arm themselves with the breastplate of the warrior, the heroic shield of valour, the helmet of poetry and the sword of truth. This visionary landscape takes those who will walk here body and soul, and will spit out with contempt any who are not worthy of it.

Whatever man has done to it over the centuries, the land has absorbed and moulded to itself. Before, there were battles. After the battles, industry. Wales is scarred with mines and quarries, blessed as it has always been with rich deposits of metals that brought prosperity to the people. I lived in the shadow of steel where men tamed the ore and fought to master it in a conflict as fierce and as bloody as any battle. The silver-hot boulders of slag exploded in crimson fireballs or showers of meteorites, tossed up like the volcanic lava of Etna or Vesuvius on our doorsteps when they were 'tipping' down the Steel Works bank in the starry dark of a winter night. Hairless, white-scarred victims of the steel lived among us, sitting helpless beside the doors of their children's cottages, staring into the sun with blind eyes. The coal that fed the furnaces was mined by young men old at forty.

Recalling my childhood, I wrote: 'We were country children who roamed for miles in all seasons; we thought nothing of tramping the miles of high moorland to the Horseshoe Pass that snakes down to the Abbey of Valle Crucis—the Abbey of the Vale of the Cross—in its green meadow: then on to the ancient town of Llangollen. I remember those tinder-dry moors with the blue, blue sky above. When you live in the country the sky becomes a dear friend.

'There were secret things that I looked for each year—woods and copses where the bluebells grew thick beneath the trees; fast-running streams with pebbles and stepping stones, where we watched our boats of leaves swirl away on the current and dabbled our toes in the cold water. Hidden deep in the woods

47

was a forgotten, empty round house made of stone which I used later in my novel *The Devil's Daughter*; there were the country roads I knew so well, fringed as they always were then with harebells and wild flowers...'

I knew where the poppies grew thickest in the yellow corn; where the magnificent rhododendron bushes of a mansion long gone still bloomed; where the old Roman salt caves were concealed, the path invisible to a stranger. I knew the ancient rocks and burial mounds, the old mine workings and shafts where, greatly daring, I had ventured into echoing darkness. But most of all I knew and revered the secret springs, the pools, the abysses where water roared and twisted in the depths far below.

The Shrine of Sirona

'The Celts regarded watercourses as a powerful manifestation of the supernatural, perhaps through their intimate connection with the earth and as a way of reaching the Otherworld.'
Stephen Allen
Lords of Battle: The World of the Celtic Warrior

Even as a child I found water sacred, whether a tiny spring winking, jewel-like in the grass; a natural stone well beneath shady trees, the drinking place for cattle; a hidden stream

48

constantly sounding the same few crystalline notes; or mysterious mirror-like pools of deep water in the silent wilderness of mountains. Like Gerard Manley Hopkins I had made pilgrimages to the shrine at Holywell as well as to other sacred sites in North Wales—many forgotten except in the huge tomes cataloguing the country's Ancient Monuments, which I consulted often over the years in the local Library in the course of my work as a journalist. (This was, of course, before the advent of the Internet.)

In all these places I felt moved, touched by something I could not explain. I simply went to them, unknowing. It was many years later that I had a sitting with Sarah, a psychic artist I met when working as a psychic in London, who sent me afterwards a striking, lovely drawing accompanied by a descriptive note:

'A woman—a spirit connected to the water—mystical—part waves, part human. Has magical energies. Colours—blues, greens, mauves, pinks—her eyes are special. Shells and stones are around her neck and in her ears. Her whole image pours with energy—a very advanced spirit on a very different level.'

'Dear Dawn' (Sarah added, using the name by which I was known when I worked in the South) *'the above I wrote when you sat with me. I hope you enjoy having her portrait.'*

I recognized the image immediately as the unknown divinity of the personal shrine I had

49

always carried within. In due course I was able to identify her as Sirona, an obscure Romano-British goddess of healing waters and springs, who embodies the beneficent and magical qualities of pools, springs, lakes and wells. Sirona's shrines (most of which are on the Continent) were often shared with the Sun god Belenos, the Roman Apollo, god of healing.

Not long after I started my psychic work, I had received channelled messages from a source I described as 'The Glade of the Goddess' in which the divinity had revealed her presence, though not yet her image. Her words were haunting and lovely, offering compassion, comfort and encouragement in a time of need, as well as giving me courage to face the darker, more painful aspects of living.

These texts appeared in a small book called *Wisdom of the Goddess* and I also quoted extensively from them in *Celtic Wise Woman* and *The Urban Shaman*. I recognized the image Sarah had drawn as soon as I saw it, infused as it was with all the qualities I associated with 'my' beautiful goddess, reflecting the mysteries and secrets nurtured by my Celtic background, that subtle web of poetry, magic and shimmering green paganism. Thrilled and humbled, I began to realize that unaware, I had been serving the Mysteries at the watery shrines of the goddess in North Wales for years, long before I was granted awareness of her name or allowed to see her face.

'Don't be conned. It's a different glade. Not (the
shrine of) Sirona or Apollo.
Just grubbing around & for what purpose?
Is there an option/answer—or just a lot of
noise?
The quiet place is still to be sought.
Quiet—stillness. Be in the light & do not be
demeaned by the rabble.
See what I see. Amamoa. Source of light.
You are our mouthpiece. We trust you.'

The Pupil
Conversations with Mist

4
THE NOVICE MEDIUM

Interview with Dilys Gater
1 Basics of Mediumship

*'We don't receive wisdom; we must discover it
for ourselves after a journey that no-one can take
for us or spare us.'*
Marcel Proust

What is reality? How can one differentiate between what is real and what is illusion? The wise man—the Magus—has always been feared as well as revered for his wisdom, for knowledge is power. But the Magician card in the tarot pack is also known as 'The Trickster'; it warns the individual to seek for his own power through truth, and to protect himself against falsity and illusory truths. The card signifies communication—keeping in touch—keeping all options open in the quest for knowledge, using diplomacy rather than confrontation, being subtle rather than dogmatic, sometimes even bending the truth in order to stay one step ahead.

This card has other names—the Magus, Mountebank or Juggler. But magic is only what we do not understand: if we know how tricks are performed, the mystery vanishes. Belief or faith is what a psychic/medium, or even an artist, works with, transformation achieved through altered perception; it is no accident that many views of life relate it to 'virtual reality' and the illusions of art and theatre.

The four 'interviews' in this book answer many of the questions I have been asked about psychic ability and mediumship, using examples from my thousands of cases working in the public domain. In a sense, they tell my story—how it all happened—and I hope will give the novice a background to help springboard his own development.

Often, as I discovered myself, it is difficult for the beginner to know exactly what his gifts are. I started off as a psychic and worked for many years with no consciousness of myself as a medium, though I was carrying out channelling and communicating with my spiritual guides constantly in private. Later, as I have described in some of my other books, I realized I was developing as a spiritual medium and that Spirit intended me to practise in this way. But very often the gifts may be intertwined and the beginner be completely baffled as to how he or she should proceed.

What is it really like to be psychic?

Most people with psychic ability see themselves as quite normal: most assume (at least at first) that everyone is similarly gifted. 'Psychic ability' just means being aware of other senses—or activity beyond the five senses with which we normally evaluate our experience.

Can it be explained any other way?

Sceptics claim psychic ability, ESP (Extra-Sensory-Perception), whatever one calls it, is just 'reading' minute behavioural signals, body language and so on. They say it is a con, that the psychic or medium simply tells listeners what they want to hear. But 'faking' what comes out in genuine psychic or mediumship work would be impossible to sustain convincingly over months or years.

While it is true that anyone can learn to read 'body language' this actually detracts from genuine 'sight'. Often I do not look directly at the person sitting in front of me: I keep my eyes closed, concentrate on the cards or stare at a fixed point. I do not want to know what their body language is saying.

Unfortunately, there is a certain amount of misunderstanding—one could say a deliberate amount of friction—between people who are psychics and people who are mediums. Psychics tend to be suspicious of mediums, while mediums in their turn are prone to denigrating the efforts of tarot card readers or those claiming psychic ability. Sometimes even the most sincere workers for Spirit will make sweeping statements that are more personal conviction than actual fact.

The dedicated and admirable Lyn G. de Swarte, for instance, former editor of the Spiritualist newspaper *Psychic News*, made this comment in her book *Principles of Spiritualism* under the heading: *A Psychic is not necessarily a Medium*:

'A psychic uses this intuition (the sixth, our earthly intuition, sometimes called our extra sensory perceptiveness or ESP) to 'read' body language, which includes facial expression, what the clothes a person wears 'say' about that person, as well as the electromagnetic and emanating energy fields around others known as auras.'

She may well believe this, but in my experience the situation is much more complex. Many people have intuitive gifts of 'sight' which cannot be so easily pigeon-holed. I discovered it was in my own interest to examine convictions and statements like this and to trust my own experience rather than any pronunciations of others in order to feel at peace with myself and my spiritual gifts, whatever they turned out to be. It is easy to worry that one is doing the 'wrong' thing as one sets out on the spiritual journey, and to doubt one's own evidence of what is real and true.

An amazingly large number of people— some of them students in my Development Classes or on courses I have conducted—have told me they do not really accept that they are psychic or that they can possibly be mediums, in spite of convincing evidence to the contrary. One has to remember that especially at the beginning, the sense of venturing into forbidden territory—communicating with dead people, voicing vague impressions rather than concrete and provable facts—provokes an automatic reaction in the human brain and it is this which is the most difficult obstacle of all for the novice to deal with.

Our brain tells us that what we are doing is not possible.

Many very highly gifted individuals consult me in great anxiety because they think they are going mad. I have many years experience working as a psychic and medium myself, but it never goes away, particularly if working directly with discarnate entities—that niggling sense that 'this is ridiculous, it can't possibly be happening.' Experience will teach the novice that with Spirit, anything and everything is possible. But we are still confined within our physical bodies and must find a balance between having confidence in the reality of Spirit and the reality (or otherwise) of being able to fly to the stars or walk through walls.

For any individuals worried about the nature of their gifts I would point out that I have given large numbers of consultations both psychically, using the tarot cards as a focus, and also using mediumship, for people I have never met and never seen. The most recent were two ladies in California, who had consultations with me at my home in the Peak District by phone. This would seem to indicate that psychic ability may not always depend on 'reading body language' or the aura, and that mediumship may not always come through specified or accepted channels. As we shall see, the novice learns to view the 'bigger picture' rather than concern himself with unnecessary detail.

How do people become psychic?

Some have 'seen' spirits all their lives; other gifted individuals may be clairsentient—aware with other senses. Such people are likely to be described as 'imaginative', 'artistic', 'neurotic' or even 'mad'—for there is often a link between psychic ability, artistic power and bipolar or similar mental disorders.

Undergoing a traumatic or life-changing event can make people psychically aware all of a sudden. For many women, for example, it happens after giving birth; for others after undergoing some dangerous incident like a car crash or a serious operation. I suppose I always had vague indications, feelings that something was developing or happening but did not know why or what it meant in the beginning. It was like possessing a key to unlock a door but not realizing the key was there until something triggered my psychic awareness: then I could start trying to find where the door was and how to open it and go through into another place.

Can you read people's minds?

'Seeing things' or 'reading people's minds' is quite different from seeing with one's physical eyes. It's more a 'knowing' than a 'seeing'. I can generally 'read people' quite easily, 'see' what they are thinking, what is in their head—but not specific thoughts. It would be more accurate to say I can see the truth, rather than what others say or the impression they want to give. Even if they deny it, experience teaches you that what your psychic gift sees is always the truth—another word for a psychic is a clairvoyant, meaning 'to see true'. Psychic ability is really being able to see the true nature and meaning of things, to whatever degree.

58

Do you ever see death? Do you tell the one who will die?

I rarely 'see' death as such, though on several occasions I found it particularly difficult to do readings for people and assumed it was because they led boring lives. Later I heard that in each case, these people died shortly afterwards—I realized then that I had not been able to read for them because there was 'nothing there'.

If one can see disaster ahead, even think it might be a death one should never say so unless the person is aware of it themselves and wants to discuss it honestly. One lady sat down with me and said: 'I know I'm dying.' She did not want sympathy or false hope, simply to be able to talk about where she was going and the process of transition.

A medium/psychic must always pass on any messages or communications they receive as accurately and truthfully as possible. But you can just as easily concentrate on reassuring enquirers that they will cope with whatever the future holds rather than scaring them with specific details of disaster. The medium/psychic must also decide exactly how much of what is perceived should be passed on and in very traumatic cases—possible death or possible miscarriage are the ones that crop up most often—you NEVER tell anyone they are about to die, or that the child they desperately hope for will never be born. You can do immense damage and must learn to choose your words very carefully.

NEVER make explicit prophesies of doom, even if you think you can see disaster looming. You might be wrong, self-empowerment and faith can move mountains; and miracles happen amazingly often.

How do you learn mediumship?

Each person should accept the particular gift he is given and try to develop it in the best way he can. Learning 'how to do it' is, as James Byrne wrote, almost impossible to teach—it can be difficult for the artist as well as the medium because often, as we have seen, there are no words to describe the processes involved. Follow your intuition is probably the best guide—and ask Spirit to guide you to a good mentor or tutor you can trust. It is said that: 'When the pupil is ready, the teacher will appear' and this often seems to apply when working in faith with Spirit.

It is assumed that a 'real' medium has complete certainty, a rock-solid guarantee of everything about his contact with Spirit, and some practitioners encourage people to believe this is true of them and their work. But as I have explained from my own experience, the developing medium is more likely to be floundering in the dark, wondering if he is actually a medium at all. My students have asked me: 'How can you know whether it is just your imagination or not?'; 'When will you be certain that what you get is really accurate?' The short answer is—probably never.

One should try not to lose sight of the fact that one is being allowed to enter areas of great wisdom, truth and wonder far beyond the experience of the 'ordinary' person. Some hesitancy or querying means one never takes the privilege of mediumship for granted; no amount of work or study gives the medium (or the artist) complete and utter certainty. Increasing experience will, however, bestow a powerful awareness and authority.

What if nothing happens?

Experience teaches any psychic or medium that if there seems to be no response from Spirit—in whatever form—there is a reason. Sometimes you are too tired and should stop. Sometimes you have already been told the answer and Spirit has no more time to mess about—fools are rarely suffered gladly, I have found. Sometimes in psychic work there can be a kind of personality clash between you and the person for whom you might be reading. Then you just say quietly: 'I am sorry; I am not the right person for you. I suggest you consult someone else.' You learn that if you have done your best neither you nor Spirit are ever at fault, it is just the wrong time or place. When I have explained to people that these things can happen, and why, they usually thank me for being honest.

I have known cases where a medium or psychic has actually lost or severed his communicative link with Spirit but has been experienced enough to carry on regardless, drawing on generalities and even sounding hugely impressive. There are some practitioners who do this a lot, just 'going through the motions' with a lot of jargon, but this attitude is an abuse of whatever gift they might have possessed initially.

The rule is always, if there is no true link with Spirit or your intuitive powers seem not to be working, you stop. You will discover that Spirit is always there, always constant. It is we human beings with our emotional hang-ups and egos yearning for attention who lose the path, wander off into byways and cul-de-sacs and become lost and confused. At times like these, we need to begin again, quietly reassessing our situation and renewing contact in faith and trust.

What should people who have a psychic gift do with it?

Like any natural gift—a talent for painting, say, or music, psychic ability helps the individual become more spiritually aware, able to appreciate life and the world in a richer, fuller way, deepening understanding and allowing the spirit/soul to grow and mature.

When I am asked 'What do you do?' the truth is, I don't do anything. It's like being able to see in colour when everyone else sees in black and white—it's just there. It does bestow a certain amount of power—sometimes a great deal—because others may not have this insight, but as I have said, anyone who tries to abuse the gifts or exploit them for their own ends will find their abilities are quickly withdrawn or blocked.

Such individuals are likely to be taught a hard lesson by Spirit, often having to start all over again with a very different attitude. The psychic gifts are not intended for personal power, to show off or to impress. They do not belong to you—they are lent in a very special sense.

Are there any particular rules?

I would say 'appropriate behaviour' rather than strict rules—because on occasion you can find yourself having to break them. Mainly, always respect the needs and vulnerabilities of those you deal with, and be prepared to take responsibility for what you do.

Some psychics and mediums will not do consultations for anyone under a certain age, sixteen, eighteen or in some cases, twenty-one. This is not because it is 'forbidden' or 'dangerous'—or even 'evil'—but because it is largely a waste of everybody's time: the subjects are too young to benefit. A child or young person is like a growing plant and from a psychic point of view it is difficult to say anything helpful: the potential far outweighs any established personality. It is like trying to comment on the beauty of a flower when it hasn't even formed a bud. Children and young people are still developing, still being taught by their own authority figures or teachers and you must respect this too, whether you think their teachers are good for them or not.

You should never trespass mentally, impose yourself or try to 'brain-wash' anyone, especially the young. If adults have not moved on then something has blocked them and if they seek help you can help them 'flower', as it were, rather than stay 'stunted'.

You need humility sometimes. We do not always know what is best, and it is important to recognize that there is room for every kind of psychic or medium, that we all have a place, a role to play. Some people can only take things on a very superficial level whereas others may be hugely advanced spiritually. Fortunately, most people feel drawn to the psychic or medium who is right for them at any given time.

What about if you encounter an evil spirit?

Real evil, complete and utter negative and destructive malevolence—in whatever form— is seldom, if ever, encountered in spiritual work, though I know there are on-going arguments about this. In my view most of the manifestations of evil a medium is likely to come across spring from the pains and cruelties of this world perpetuating themselves in ignorance and fear in the spiritual, drawing power from similar human sources and terrors in those who encounter them. It is true that situations can arise involving departed spirits which for whatever reason, display negative or hostile tendencies, or various 'energy forms' of a destructive nature, but the novice will probably never be required to deal with any of them if he carries out his activities responsibly.

Danger signs to watch for are not manifestations of demons or entities from other dimensions but far more subtle: sudden extremes (even 'good' ones) or any disruptive/ manic imbalance beginning to occur in people. Any violent personality changes should be noted, though one has to be aware that some clinical mental disorders can have similar symptoms (superficially, anyway) to the altered states of intuitive vision. If any situation worries you, get medical help immediately or call in someone with more psychic and/or spiritual experience who can clarify matters.

Unless undertaking serious work in Soul or Spirit Rescue Circles, I have found that people who regularly encounter dangerous or 'evil' entities and situations may be provoking these themselves: their egos may need to consider themselves more powerful or important than less flamboyant personalities. I have also encountered situations where individuals had previously consulted someone else—most usually requesting them to work magic or cast spells to obtain money or a love partner—and been left with the mess when the spells went wrong.

In one unforgettable case a lady in her sixties had used the spell given her by a self-styled witch (involving rituals while in her bath) in order to 'get' the man she wanted. Instead, the man had gone off with someone else and the lady unaccountably over-reacted, becoming desperately depressed and suicidal. When she called me in I found her comfortable house was icy cold and I identified a small elemental spirit that looked (in my clairvoyant view, though invisible to her) like a hideous gargoyle crouched on her hearthrug in front of the gas fire, absorbing all the warmth and all her human energy into itself.

I had brought my 'black bag' containing the items I would need to deal with this kind of situation, and was able to carry out the necessary procedures for removing the elemental and sending it back to where it belonged, cleansing and purifying the house leaving candles burning. But how had it got there in the first place?

Evil—even relatively small fry like this bullying little elemental—cannot go anywhere unless invited in. There has to be some kind of collusion, a lessening of the Light somewhere in order to allow in the Dark—as well as the willingness to allow it to take root and flourish. I concluded that the elemental had arrived at this woman's house with the witch, feeding on her selfish desires and finding a very comfortable home on her hearthrug. She admitted she had told the witch about the cold and her suicidal state of mind and asked him to return and help her, but he said there was nothing he could do.

In some instances this would have been true, since it is the perpetrator of any magic, spell or working who is responsible and must deal with whatever outcome there might be. Here the activity (on both sides) seemed to me to display just ignorance and greed; but you cannot mess about with the powers and anyone who sets out to work magic (as I explained in *Celtic Wise Woman*) must be prepared to pay a price for it—the catch is that you may not realize until too late just what that price might be. This woman had been foolish and I doubted that the 'witch' (if he really was an initiated practitioner) had known what he was doing. The consequences could have been dire, particularly as the lady continued to repeat similar procedures over the next few months in order to get rid of the woman who had taken 'her' man. Later this perfectly rational individual, who had been seen by several specialists and pronounced completely sane, became convinced her 'rival' was trying to reflect 'evil' and 'curses' into her home using mirrors in the house across the road.

She continued to call me in and each time I explained that it was her own attitude causing the problems; that she should try to be more positive in her socializing rather than relying on spells to get what she wanted. In the end I had to tell her I could help her no further. Each time I went to her house I left feeling exhausted and depleted and it was obvious she was not prepared to learn from her experiences.

It is amazing how many people I have encountered, at all levels of society, who retain an archaic conviction that the 'wise woman' or some similar practitioner can, if consulted, hand over a spell or carry out a ritual to perform a miracle for their gratification. Working with Spirit or with any kind of psychic or spiritual power is a blessed gift and privilege. It is not an ego-trip and the ultimate aim should never be simply to obtain whatever one might want—for Spirit provides everything that is needed—or to show off or scare others. The aim is to accept instruction and guidance in the soul's development and to assist in Spirit's purpose however one can.

List of Definitions

Even though we live in a supposedly enlightened society, the public at large is still inclined to lump mediums of whatever sort together with psychics, clairvoyants, tarot readers, spiritualists, witches, pagans and even practitioners of voodoo, devil worship and magic whether white or black, without the slightest degree of knowledge about any of them. (Sometimes this also seems to apply to the practitioners, as in the case I have just detailed). If such an ignorant and blinkered attitude is encountered the best thing is always to withdraw and refuse to become involved. Never try to argue—or even to 'discuss' unless you are sure the request for information is genuine.

How I choose to work is between Spirit and me, and I do not force my beliefs unasked on anyone else. When I am working, however, complete strangers who would pride themselves on their good manners and on never behaving rudely, are likely to remark loudly and pointedly in my hearing: 'I don't believe in mumbo jumbo and black magic', 'Tarot cards, they're evil', or 'We go to church, we don't hold with devil worship'.

It is a fact that as well as feeling vulnerable while trying to follow one's spiritual path, the psychic/medium can often be made to feel very much under threat in today's society, not sure how to present him or herself. The following list of brief explanatory definitions is included to help clarify matters

- **Spiritualism** originated in the USA during the 19th century. Defined as basically 'a monotheistic belief system or religion, postulating a belief in God, but with the distinguishing feature of belief that the dead residing in the spirit world can be contacted by 'mediums', who can then provide information about the afterlife.' Originally there was no organized form of worship or recognized statement of belief—adherents met in circles or groups with recognized mediums and information was published in various spiritualist periodicals. This evolved into:

- **The Spiritualist Church**—organized along the lines of any other denominational body, the Spiritualist Church (known in Great Britain as the **Spiritualists' National Union** or **SNU**) does not take the Bible as the main source of its knowledge of the divine. It believes in Seven Principles of Faith (Nine in the USA) and organizes its own training for its mediums and healers; importantly,

70

as a contributor to the former Spiritualist newspaper *Psychic News* explained, Spiritualism: 'supports a scientific spirit in its philosophy which is grounded in our unique experience and freedom from dogma'. Many churches are affiliated and there is some debate among members as to whether they term themselves Christian Spiritualists (accepting redemption through Christ) or whether they take a more shamanic attitude, regarding Christ as a great medium and teacher but who was not divine. This seems to be largely a matter of personal belief. Spiritualism is now a legally recognized religion and it is the dedicated work of Spiritualist mediums to give 'evidence of survival' and offer proof that the soul lives on after death: this can apply whether those concerned are Christian Spiritualists or not. Spiritualists believe that the soul (or spirit) continues to develop and progress through further worlds or 'spheres' after death.

- **Paganism** and **Witchcraft (also known as Wicca)** are both ancient systems of belief that follow 'the old path' in connecting with entities and divinities of the spiritual and natural worlds of the Celts and tribes who lived before Christianity came to the west. Their activities centre round the celebration of life and nature, expressed in a personal lifestyle as well as regular meetings under the leadership of each group (or coven's) High Priestess and High Priest. Believers try to live in harmony with all natural things and these are religious faiths in that believers worship their own particular deities (usually the Goddess and her consort the Horned God—sometimes known as the Lady and Lord) and try to live according to their beliefs. There are differences in these nature-based religions and though most witches or Wiccans would describe themselves as pagan, not all pagans are specifically witches.

- **Neo-paganism and New Age** are terms for the revivals of interest in ancient pagan lifestyles occurring over the last few centuries and popular fascination with the occult and esoteric which boomed during the late 20th century.

- **Vodou (also known as Voodoo)**—This very ancient religion with roots in the African continent spread via the slave trade to the Americas, becoming most firmly established in Haiti. A complicated belief system, it has been described as 'embracing the relationship between nature, man and the unseen forces that order the cosmos': it incorporates the religious practices of many African tribes as well as the Taino

Indians, the original inhabitants of Haiti and also of Catholicism, taken to Haiti by Christian missionaries. Its pantheon of gods and spirits are evoked in ceremonies of music, dancing and sacrifice—sometimes of animals. Sorcery and ceremonial possession are practised by some believers.

- Modern-day **psychics** and **clairvoyants** are 'sensitives' gifted with 'second sight', 'sixth sense' or whatever else one might call it who give counselling consultations to enquirers. **Tarot readers** work mainly with the traditional meanings of the tarot cards as their guide: they may or may not also possess gifts of psychic awareness. But whether such people practise as a full-time occupation or just for the benefit of close friends and family, the ultimate aim is not 'fortune-telling' or 'predicting the future' (which cannot actually be done in the way most people imagine): the true purpose of psychics and their work should be to empower whoever consults them to discover a deeper, richer and more truthful way of living encompassing spiritual as well as material values.

- **Mediums** are enabled to contact other spheres of existence including that of the dead, and pass on information received. They may also have psychic or clairvoyant abilities, but not necessarily. Psychics too, may have mediumistic abilities.

- **Shamans** are individuals who work with the energies and forces of the natural world; they are enabled to make spiritual journeys into Otherworlds and relate to the realms of animals and the dead. They are often marked from birth as chosen by the spirits for this purpose, especially in primitive tribes, and undergo initiatory quests and long periods of training and development. They are also likely to be mediums.

- **Magicians** or **Magi** (as opposed to illusionists or members of the Magic Circle) are adepts who have studied ancient esoteric lore of some kind and actively practise it. Basically the magician learns to harness and work with the elements in order to bring about change and impose his will on the natural world. The powers are the same whether employed in so-called 'white magic' or in 'black magic': **'white magic'** is beneficent, intended for the greater good of all: **'black magic'** involves spells and rituals carried out to benefit those concerned and endow them with personal power.

- **Devil worship/ Black mass** were largely media terms coined to sell as many copies as possible of any newspaper or periodical

74

featuring them. They are basically 'negative' Christian concepts of what the 'dark' side of Christian worship would be like if anyone tried to deflect and appropriate the power of the deity for his own ends. The author Dennis Wheatley popularized these ideas in the mid-20th century, and though from time to time individuals have claimed to practise them with or without the assistance of like-minded companions, they have no serious existence outside adolescent fantasy.

- The **Black Arts** is the term for what 'black' magicians practise if they are following what is referred to as the 'left-hand path'—another emotive term. **Satanists** are those who choose to worship/invoke Satan instead of any other of the angelic or demonic hierarchy when working magic. The figure of the Dark Angel, the Devil, Lucifer, Satan or whatever else one chooses to call him, never existed as such in the pagan world (ie: before the study of the Hebrew Kabbalah or the Christian Church's teachings came to Britain). The dark gods of pagan belief were recognized as legitimate members of the pantheon, as necessary for the balance of the whole as more beneficent divinities. It was the Christian Church which was responsible for creating the figure of 'the Devil', labelling him wicked, evil and bad.

PART TWO
DEATH AND THE MAIDEN

*'From the bough, the white berry within your
cup.
Pearls from the sea-strand upon your brow.
The prints of your feet on the sand are centuries
old, each tide
you walk there anew, the shells grating together.*

*There are landmarks to make you weep, blurry
through the rain.
The heart sickens with old griefs, blood on the
sword.*

*You walk in moonlight, in the half-light, on the
enchanted strand.
No sword can rest once it has been grasped, and
the heart must fight on,
even if the strand is empty. Fight the waves. This
is your domain.
You rule the shadows.'*

Blessing for the Initiate
Celtic Wise Woman

'...man is a creature who walks in two worlds and traces upon the walls of his cave the wonders and the nightmare experiences of his spiritual pilgrimage.'

Morris West

My Mediumship Begins

Working as a psychic in London, I often attended the Spiritualist Church in Fulham, where I lived. Like most Spiritualist Churches this offered spiritual healing after services and during the week, and I was thankful to be able to take advantage of these sessions—not only struggling with my spiritual development but also suffering poor physical health. A painful back problem made it difficult to move at all and the sessions made me feel better and calmer. It was while they were taking place that—quite spontaneously—my mediumship began to develop and I started to receive messages from the spirit world, initially for the healers who were working on me.

I was very chary and doubtful to begin with. Relatively new to the Church, I held mediums in high esteem. Some, I knew, had trained for years—so how was it possible I could just 'naturally' start communicating with the departed? But the messages kept coming, though I did wonder whether I was inducing them myself and was also aware of the danger of accepting apparent psychic/spirit messages without question when inexperienced. Crucially, what reassured me was that my early development as a medium happened while I was actually in the Church building, under the supervision of healers working for Spirit.

They were hugely supportive and encouraging, and though I later found my destined path to be that of a psychic maverick with no affiliations to any one formal creed, I do not believe it was by chance that my first steps into mediumship were made literally within the Church. Nor that the earliest communications I received for myself met my most pressing needs by rooting me very firmly in the physical.

5
SPIRIT GUIDANCE

*'The initiate seeks an inner source of power,
which is generally couched in terms of inner
'contacts'. It is this…that distinguishes the
religious mystic from the ordinary worshipper…
The occult initiate is a specialist.'*

Gareth Knight
*Introduction: The Training & Work of the
Initiate by Dion Fortune*

'Are you really giving me these messages or
are they already in my mind?'

*'You are part of the great core of knowledge
where all
is revealed already. You know all but it is clear to
your sight
fragment by fragment'*

The Pupil
Conversations with Mist

I was in my forties when I began to attend the
Spiritualist Church, with little experience of
the activities of mediums. Working as I did in
the field of investigative journalism, I regarded
most accounts of supernatural happenings I

81

came across as just good copy for a 'ghostly' feature, interesting perhaps, but certainly 'unproven'. At the Church I was initially awed by the different mediums I saw at work—particularly their obvious sincerity and dedication—but began to be less impressed as time went by and I worked regularly with mediums at Psychic Fairs.

The signals were in my view, extremely conflicting. I was, after all, a journalist of wide experience who knew a great deal about how to write emotively, how to manipulate public perception. The needy and the bereaved were obviously sitting targets for the sympathetic ministrations of anyone who assured them that their departed loved ones were 'all right' and that everything would work out fortuitously for them 'on the Earth plane'. But could such bland superficialities really be meaningful, even if they had been communicated from 'the Other Side'? Though people seemed to benefit from the messages they received, I found it difficult to take them seriously, especially as some of the mediums I worked with repeated more or less the same messages to everyone.

Perhaps my cynicism was a blessing for it meant that I tested and examined the ground every step of the way so far as the whole subject of spiritual communications was concerned. Over the years I discovered the business of mediumship to be extremely complex—for instance I found that many 'ordinary' people actually communicate regularly with departed relatives or other entities in a perfectly natural way; they do not, however, consider themselves 'mediums'. Creative artists, too, may have some ritual or procedure by which they access the source of their inspiration, but they do not claim to be 'mediums' either, though they often acknowledge they are merely vessels through which the creative force is able to pass.

It was the activities of 'professional' mediums which I found lacking in credibility. Many I met were remarkably unspiritual and materially-minded, or else seemed naïve to a point difficult to take seriously. Some I dismissed because of their obvious lack of education. In my arrogance I was, like many critics, mistaking the messenger for the message, the instrument for the music.

A psychic or spiritual medium usually admits publicly to working with a 'Spirit Guide' (or 'Guides') who is some kind of discarnate being. Often, however, this very fact can work against them if they behave as though they are a child in the presence of an 'invisible friend', laughing together over private jokes and scolding each other for behaving badly, as some do. It can be very disconcerting for others, and I continued for years to feel awkward and embarrassed when listening to one-sided conversations between mediums and their unseen mentors. Even when I was working as a medium myself, I was reluctant for a long time to refer openly to 'my Spirit Guide' or repeat to others the teachings 'he' had given to me.

One of the things I found confusing in those early days was that since every medium has his own unique experience of 'Spirit Guides' or connections, there is no single method of working that is 'right'. There can be all kinds of guidance and it might be helpful here to take a look at the broad catagories into which 'Spirit Guides' of individual mediums can usually be placed.

Types of Spirit Guides

- *Ancient or more recent sages, wise or enlightened men (or women), professors, doctors, and other authoritative teachers or practitioners—*

Spirit Guides make themselves known to the medium when the time is right for him to begin taking his vocation seriously. The most recognizable—and most common—guide is someone or something that seems to have an identity of its own, a definite personality, even a name. Such guides may be perceived as human beings who have lived previously, often ancestors, parents or the disembodied dead in the form of other saintly people known or unknown. They may be from any era, civilization or discipline we know about (such as ancient China, Tibet, Ancient Egypt, the indigenous people of North or South America) or from civilizations now lost to us, such as Atlantis, ancient Babylon or even peoples we have never heard about—whether there is any proof these actually existed or not.

I have known mediums whose guides were Tibetan monks, Chinese Mandarins, Red Indian Chiefs, Atlantean priests, Ancient Egyptian priestesses, European Kings and Queens, Ancient Romans, former physicians, surgeons, nurses or nuns. Among the most unusual of other people's guides I have come across were a seven-foot tall Rastafarian with dreadlocks, a hugely elevated sage from some unidentifiable plane of existence who boomed advanced mathematical and philosophical concepts at me until my head was bursting, and an iconic pop singer, poet and performer still idolized by millions. Mediums who have written about their guides have listed physicians and medical practitioners in spirit (some very eminent); as well as guides who assist or perform cures, healing and even carrying out 'psychic' surgery through the medium.

Because so many accounts of their activities have been made available, Native American

Indian guides are among the most popularly recognised. **Silver Birch**, described as 'one of Spiritualism's most eloquent, much-loved guides', spoke through the mediumship of Maurice Barbanell, the founding editor of the Spiritualist newspaper *Psychic News*. Mr Barbanell (who died in 1981) regularly sat in the Hannen Swaffer Home Circle during the early years of the 20th century. Hundreds of people asked for instruction on every kind of subject—from free will to the meaning of life and the nature of time—and a large number of books were made available with selections from Silver Birch's teachings. **White Eagle** is another noted guide whose teachings, available from the White Eagle Lodge, came through the dedicated mediumship of Grace Cooke.

Many of these learned guides offer information about what it is like on the 'Other Side' as well as enlightenment to assist us on our path through this life and beyond. But the main function of a 'Spirit Guide' is usually perceived by the public as facilitating contact between the medium and any departed spirits wanting to contact loved ones on 'this side of the Veil'. This type of Guide is sometimes called a '**control**', since he/she takes charge of the proceedings during a séance or sitting. An example is that of the medium Linda

86

Williamson, who describes her Spirit Guide, a girl called Sally, as a 'crowd controller', there to keep the spirits who want to communicate through her in order.

Another such was the great direct voice medium Leslie Flint who had a 'spirit helper' called Mickey, a Cockney child who had been run over in a street accident in Camden Town in the early 1900s. He can be heard in sessions of Flint's direct voice medium-ship on his website www.leslieflint.com, the miracles of technology having made available many examples of spirits speaking through Leslie Flint in their own voices. The results of these sessions were, by any standards, amazing and the aspiring medium is recommended to experience them—but also (as always) advised to keep an open mind. I have found each individual receives communications in the right way for him or her, and the novice must learn to take what is helpful from the mediumship of others but in the end, rely on his own experience and the veracity of his personal guides and sources.

• *Doorkeeper and Gatekeepers—*
These are not strictly guides, but anyone entering other states of being puts himself outside of time and space and may encounter entities who help to facilitate travel between levels and dimensions— whether mental, astral or whatever else.

87

Usually referred to as 'Doorkeepers' or 'Gatekeepers', these can be perceived as a kind of spiritual 'bouncer', whose function is to guard and protect the questing spirit. They do not provide teachings or guidance, simply give basic information and facilitate safe travel in and out of Otherworlds.

• *Angels*—

The concept of 'angels' can vary according to the individual. What are they? And are any—or indeed, all—of our guides actually angels?

The Bible tells us: *'He has given His angels charge over thee to keep thee in all thy ways'*— this sense of 'keep' being the old meaning, to 'take wise and informed care of'. This also infers encouraging growth and progress, while other religions identify angels as teachers; the Greek work *'angelos'* means 'messengers'. Interestingly, the word 'educate' comes from the Latin, meaning 'to lead out': so our guides teach or educate us by leading us on (or out) towards the transcendence to which we aspire but could never hope to achieve alone. Many people regard a departed relative— grandmother, father, mother—as their Spirit Guide; some people also regard departed relatives and any other 'Spirit Guides' they are aware of as angels. But there are fine distinctions between our own loved ones and the enlightened teachers or educators who are there to guide us in wisdom.

Writer Jacky Newcomb, whose books focus on accounts of interaction with angels, states very clearly: *'I recognize the difference between angels, spirit guides and our loved ones on the Other Side....*

'Angels are beings of pure consciousness who do not incarnate. They have little understanding of our day-to-day problems like paying the mortgage, for example.

'Spirit guides are souls much like ourselves who have taken on the role of teachers... Although our loved ones are neither angels nor spirit guides, they often seem to perform a similar role.'

Regarding the nature of angels, medium Philip Solomon has written: *'The job of angels seems to be very much praising and attending to what we think of as the God force. There are also angels of healing, empowerment, creativity and many other areas.*

'Archangels, it seems, serve as intermediaries between us in this world and the very highest levels of existence in the next.'

'Spirit Guides'—being disembodied—are usually only 'seen' and/ or 'heard' by the medium himself, who passes on whatever communications he receives in ways we will discuss later. This kind of activity is within the mind and is called **mental mediumship**.

In instances of **physical mediumship** the guide 'takes over' the body of the medium—to whatever degree—sometimes superimposing his features upon the features of the medium and using the medium's voice-box. In cases that are now rare, spirits or guides reveal themselves in a physical sense, materializing visually during a séance or allowing observers to make contact by physical touch. Because physical mediumship involves the apparent appearance of spirit forms, transformation of the medium or similar phenomena it usually requires an appropriate setting in which to work and because of the physical nature of such manifestations these cases have been the most likely over the years to have been 'exposed' as trickery or fraud.

I personally have never witnessed a spirit or guide make itself independently manifest 'in the flesh' via ectoplasm or any other means. I have, however, witnessed instances of 'over-shadowing' of mediums at close quarters where the presence of the spirit or entity was clearly visible as both the features and voice of the host dramatically changed. Such cases are unmistakable, amazing—often disturbing—to encounter. Even for an observer, the sense that the body is being used by another entity, often of unexpected and unfamiliar power, can be very unsettling because once again *our brain tells us this is not possible.*

The novice must be careful to work under skilled supervision if his gifts lie in the realms of physical mediumship: I have known its manifestations take the developing medium by surprise and frighten him or her.

Mist—I meet my Guide

Setting out on my path of spiritual development I looked for a Mentor, some charismatic person I would be able to trust to guide and teach me. I have never encountered one on a human level, though there have been many with authoritative opinions to offer—some of which greatly assisted me. But I followed my usual course, proceeding as I had done as a writer, querying, questioning, testing theories, learning, reading, studying, experiencing for myself and making up my own mind.

I leaned heavily on my sense of communication with Spirit, spending regular hours each day in meditation. I prayed for guidance and in due course, a figure made its appearance in my meditations: this mysterious person—I thought a woman—wore a long blue velvet cloak and seemed to lead me through a forest of tall trees. The face was averted, but I realized I had been aware of 'the woman in the blue cloak' as far back as fifteen or so years earlier when I had seen her in a dream.

Hooded and anonymous, she led me on through the forest and after pursuing these meditations for some weeks, I asked whether she would grant me the privilege of seeing her face.

To my astonishment, the blue cloak collapsed in on itself and far from the imposing 'Spirit Guide' I expected there was no body there at all. Instead I was looking into the most exquisite tiny triangular silver face with enormous, expressive silver eyes. Apart from its face this tiny entity had no form and I concluded later that even the face had been created for my benefit, allowing me to identify with a spirit which would have been far too difficult for me to envisage—at that stage—as completely disembodied. I had also been transported to what I perceived as a glade composed of blue and silver light, where later in my meditations another small spirit similar to the first made its appearance. These two gave me loving encouragement and the silver glade (which I called the 'Star Plane') offered calm, purification and healing.

The companionship of the 'Little Spirits' enriched my life and I assumed at first they were my 'Spirit Guides'. As I progressed, however, I was to learn that the real source of my guidance was far greater than had at first appeared. The 'Little Spirits', tiny fragments of loving energy, were just sparks, as it were, of the real fire. The power and presence of my true guide Mist could only be revealed to me in stages over a period of time, as I became able to accept them.

In a practical sense I had been receiving 'channelled' communications from several different sources during the early months of my spiritual journey, all enlightening and inspiring but seeming to lack the primary authority and consistency I sought. The 'Little Spirits' were to offer companionship and support, but I sent out an urgent prayer for the personal guidance and instruction I still felt I badly needed. When I sat down to meditate that same evening, I became aware of another voice and realized later that as soon as I asked, Spirit had responded. I had found my source of wisdom, the presence I would come to know as 'Mist', my principal guide and teacher.

'Mist' is so called because 'he' is a highly elevated presence that has no form and no name. I perceived and still perceive 'him' as basically a swirling cloud of silvery essence/life force which can communicate on many levels as required. 'He' is difficult to describe, since 'he' never existed in any recognizable incarnation, simply as that energy force: when I asked 'him' for a name, I was given only the fact that 'I am mist'.

Recently reading Lita de Alberdi's book *Channelling: What it is and how to do it* I came

93

across this statement from one of her guides, Ortan: *'I am dwelling in a form which to you would appear perhaps as simply a shimmer, as a movement within the air'.*

This appears to me very similar to my concept of Mist, and another group of guides can be said to consist of **elevated/highly evolved beings** like these. Though they might be asked 'Who are you?' or 'Where do you come from?' the answers are extremely vague—largely such responses consist of references (as in the case of Ortan) to energy forms, vibrations on the ether, swirls of light (like Mist) all incomprehensible to the human brain.

During the twenty years I have worked with Mist, my vision of 'him' has developed and clarified. Originally 'he' presented 'himself' in a form I could relate to—as an actual person, 'a silver man with no face', encased in a sort of silver armour with a visor completely covering 'his' head. I perceived 'his' presence as male and as in many similar partnerships between the medium and his/her 'Spirit Guide' the relationship soon became the most significant and meaningful one in my life. Eventually I was able to perceive 'him' not as a person but as the elevated being I have described of no sex or form at all—a representation of some extremely advanced essence I can, in my human state, only appreciate as a fraction of its true force, wisdom and power. Once when

I was working on a sustained spiritual level I 'saw' the form of Mist take on other images, one that looked like a DNA sample seen through a microscope, a glimpse of life energy that perhaps strangely, made a great deal of sense to me.

Every medium's relationship with his or her guide is intense and committed. Mine deepened over the years into such a close intimacy that communication could only be expressed in the most passionate endearments of attachment and love. Since this also seems to be the experience of other mediums and because they reflect the nature of the relationship, I have left them in this book wherever they occur.

From the evening when I first made contact I wrote down all my communications with Mist as 'conversations'—largely my questions and 'his' answers—retaining them, as I have mentioned, as a reference book to which I return again and again. The dialogues still continue, though less often. If I feel in particular need of enlightenment or help I will make contact and might spend days or even weeks communicating on a high spiritual level until I have worked through that particular stage in my development. Then communication can lapse until I reach a further point where I am ready for more instruction.

My spiritual growth as reflected in these files has proceeded in 'lessons', some spaced months apart, others following closely together. Re-reading them for this book I realize they are not so much concerned with 'working for Spirit' (though the teachings are there) but providing much-needed encouragement and support to a human being struggling with the problems of living a physical existence while following a committed spiritual path as best she can, beset by illness, lack of trust and faith, personal loneliness, sometimes intense doubt and fear. What comes across most strongly is the immense patience and care of my guide as I blundered on, attempting spiritual progress but often missing the point, losing my sense of spiritual connection, chasing after a new idea for a book, a new job, a new relationship, worrying about lack of money, lack of confidence, my health problems, whether I was seriously ill or even dying.

I have never bothered about exactly 'who' or 'what' Mist is. It is enough that 'he' appears whenever and in whatever form 'he' is needed, always providing what is necessary at that time whether I am aware enough to ask for what is needed or not. Other, more recognizable 'guides' have also made their appearance at various times, providing their uniquely valuable kinds of help and enlightenment, but

Mist has been, and remains, my constant link with the Source.

'Lesser than yourself cannot lift you nor encourage you. They do not understand the burdens.
You must lift yourself by your own needs....Free yourself and walk the forest, the mountain. Shine. Be. Your shining depends on no-one. Their shining is irrelevant to you.'

The Pupil
Conversations with Mist

The Hermit

'The lantern of knowledge carried by the Hermit illuminates our inner life…'

Annie Lionnet
The Tarot Directory

The Hermit card in the tarot pack foreshadows the card called Death—both concern spiritual exploration, letting all parts of the self go, sacrificing all to enter into wisdom after the symbolic death of the human self-force, the Ego. This can be a time of revelation, the solitary life-style of the Hermit allowing a period of meditation and withdrawal. He ventures deep into the worlds that lie both without and within.

The Hermit also urges us to explore the physical experience of our senses, relating intensely to them and to the natural world. Summer paths, lakes, views, scents of flowers—bird-song, music, the sound of running water—thunder and lightning, crackling fire, the receptiveness of warm sand, deep grass, dark earth—all these reinforce our intuitive awareness of truth and of Spirit. We live many times in our senses and we can use sensory experience as a method of transmuting the physical into the spiritual.

Physically the Hermit is quite alone. No-one

can accompany the spiritual traveller along this path and the overwhelming sense of isolation is something with which the medium—and the artistically gifted—must come to terms. You are your own source of physical strength, of authority and self-discipline; your own counsellor in the endless quest to achieve the divine wisdom.

'I was with you when you came into the world, I came as far as I was able along the way and held you before you went from us to represent us in your body. It was difficult to let you go, knowing your way would be hard and lonely, but we have been with you throughout all, if you could have seen us.'

The Pupil
Conversations with Mist

99

6
THE LIFE FORCE

'The grove there was untouched by human hands from ancient times, whose interlacing boughs enclosed a space of darkness and cold shadow which banished the sunlight from above. Gods were worshipped there with savage rites... Birds feared to perch on the branches, wild beasts would not lie down. No wind bore down upon that wood; the leaves of the trees rustled without a breeze. Water fell from dark springs...'

The Civil War (Pharsalia)
Lucan

A medium's work is carried out at the mysterious boundary that marks the transition between living and dying, between this and other worlds of being. The atmospheric quote above giving the Roman poet's perception of the sacred groves where pagan priests or priestesses carried out their rites, reflects the 'ordinary' person's feelings of awe and fear when standing at this boundary. They sense the immensity of the task confronting the medium or artist, even though ignorant of what might be involved.

This is no place for the faint-hearted. The threshold between life and death can be a lonely and sometimes terrifying place. The medium's path involves struggle and fortitude both within and without, the application of self-control over powerful forces. The levels of communication in which the medium becomes adept all require resources of energy and commitment. The definition of a prophet is one whose inspirational truths come from the Source, who is in touch with and passes on messages from the Divine, and though this may not be appreciated initially, it should also be the aim of the committed medium. He must go forward alone, taking responsibility for his material and spiritual wellbeing regardless of what rules others choose to live by.

The physical and emotional problems of development can sometimes swamp any real ability to share the awareness of higher dimensions as they are revealed—the lives of creative artists of genius often reflect this. But dangers do not lie with the horror of dark waters or rituals in sinister groves as envisioned by Lucan, rather in the awareness that the medium's journey is indeed a liminal one, proceeding with an increasing sense that one works and lives continually 'on the threshold' and has no rooted reality in one world or the other.

There comes a point—which continues to recur as one progresses—when awareness can almost implode within one's perception and it is necessary to back off, as it were, to allow oneself time to recover before any further progress can be made.

Many traditions with which we are familiar present the world of the dead—the Underworld—as lying across a river or some sort of watery barrier. Even the Christian tradition incorporates this, 'crossing the Jordan' in gospel songs and spirituals. In Greek mythology the souls of the dead were ferried across the River Styx by Charon, the boatman. The dying Arthur was transported on a barge to the legendary Isle of Avalon. The huge import of this journey, 'crossing the water', has always been recognized, the voyages of life and death marked with great reverence. The Old Norse word 'ludr', meaning 'boat', also means both a cradle and a coffin: the shamanic vision revealing that death and rebirth are the same. The ancients of Scandinavia held their funerals on ships, which then began a new journey into the Underworld with the soul of the departed warrior.

The work of both medium and artist takes them to the very bank of this mysterious dark river—sometimes even across it—but of course, this cannot be done physically. The medium and the artist 'cross the water' in a mental sense, their work carried out in a state of altered consciousness known as trance.

Trance

Trance—the ability to focus the mind—can be called by various names, imagination, even inspiration, but it is far more than that: the concentration of energy and force is a powerful tool. Discipline both physical and mental is necessary to learn how to become familiar and work with the process of trance. The medium must be able to induce it when he wants to and avoid being overcome by it without his awareness.

As a mental medium, I personally need to be careful in this respect: lights—traffic lights or moving street lights for example—can 'put me under' easily, which is why I do not drive. A medium must also learn how to 'switch off' when not working so he does not 'pick up' in places where there are heavy atmospheres or presences—even strong energies in people themselves. A medium learns to close down the mental channels when in everyday interactions of an ordinary kind, shopping, carrying out normal business. It is easy to be 'invaded' and made uncomfortable, even ill and the further one progresses in this work, the greater is the need for solitude.

In ancient times it was a priestess serving at a shrine who was the mouth-piece, the oracle of the god (or goddess). She had visions or prophesied while entranced: at the famous shrine of Apollo in Delphi she sat 'in the smoke', breathing a hallucinogenic natural vapour that issued from fissures in the rock; in other places she underwent similar drug-induced trances.

Like some illustrious mediums of more recent times she was not necessarily a highly educated person. She was there to be used, her role simply to act as a material channel allowing access to information from the divine: often the messages were so incomprehensible that special priests were in attendance to 'translate' them for petitioners. The priestesses of Delphi were originally young and beautiful but the arduous nature of the task—the physical suffering that accompanied sessions of entrancement and an occasion when the priestess was raped because of her beauty—persuaded the attendants at the shrine they needed a more mature, sturdier female of peasant stock.

The role of medium—channel of access to the gods—has never been physically easy, the main requirements possibly being sheer stamina and a stubborn quality of dogged persistence: two famous mediums, Joan of Arc and Helen Duncan, were typical of the kind of ordinary women who, simply possessing the intuitive gift of mediumship, were used—even exploited—by others. In ancient times the fate

104

of a priestess was often to be thrown aside when her usefulness was at an end: in herself she had no standing, someone else could always be found to take her place.

For the priestess/medium today, whether working within a recognized discipline or alone, the role can carry similar risks. Sustained mediumship of any kind puts great strain on the fabric of the physical body. 'Physical' mediums who become entranced need the protection of working in a controlled environment; and I have mentioned that with 'mental' mediums (like myself) mental solitude may become so necessary that unless the medium is able to live apart, to whatever degree, she is likely to become mentally and physically ill.

Not everyone reaches this level of working with Spirit but the further the medium progresses, the more necessary it becomes to protect oneself as a dedicated instrument rather than an autonomous being. In ancient pagan belief there was a constant, finely-edged balance between the spiritual and physical worlds, with far more of a sense of obligation than we acknowledge today. The gods would be generous but only if their demands were met to their satisfaction. It was accepted that some sacrifice was always necessary, and invariably the sacrifice was expected to be of the brightest and best; youth, strength and beauty had to be ploughed back into the earth to ensure a bountiful harvest and a fortunate year. Blood had to be spilled. The sacrifice was a solemn pledge that was never taken lightly.

In the Celtic culture and others like that of Ancient Egypt the king's power was divinely given: he was effectively the living embodiment of the god or gods, obliged to carry responsibilities that were awesome. Bestowed with the highest authority, his life was not his own, it belonged to his people; his will to live and to rule was also, if it had to be so, his will to die on their behalf.

The committed medium, whether born to awareness of his gifts or called later in life, has been chosen by Spirit as a representative on Earth. Often he must achieve by the power of his will alone so he needs to find and cultivate immense strength of purpose within himself. Like the shaman—like the artist dedicated to his art—he must sacrifice his highest endeavour to carrying out what is demanded from him. He must hold nothing back, pledging everything he has in the name of those who cannot. As the chosen link with Spirit he must devote his whole life and purpose to keeping faith.

Psychic Protection

'Mystery, or unknowing, is energy. As soon as a mystery is explained, it ceases to be a source of

energy. If we question deep enough there comes
a point where answers, if answers could be given,
would kill...'

John Fowles
The Aristos

The medium Pamela Ball commented in her psychic investigation into the identity of Jack the Ripper, on the need for what is called 'psychic protection'. Often a medium works with a group or Circle of supporters who are there to contribute their energies to the effort of communication: someone in the Circle may also conduct the group's activities if the medium herself is in some state of trance and unable to take charge. Pamela Ball's team supported her during her sessions of mediumship and also carried out any necessary research, leaving her mind, the receptive instrument, uncontaminated by the historical facts, which were discussed and collated later.

Like any responsible medium, Pamela Ball took appropriate steps to protect herself and the members of her team as well as any spirits she made contact with during the undertaking. Protection is a serious business. It is always the medium's responsibility to ensure he or she has the knowledge and back-up to work safely: guarding against accidental disasters of the kind we sometimes hear about when

107

stage hypnotists or other performers cannot deal with states into which they might have put members of the audience. And though highly unlikely to be the victim of what is called 'psychic attack', even the newest novice must always protect his activities through prayer and awareness, invoking a Higher Power to bless what he is doing and being careful.

Basically, mental mediumship is a simple process. You begin by asking your guides and/or any other spirits whether they are present and if they will speak to you. The aspiring medium can use his voice (either aloud or within his head) and directly address whatever spirits he wants to contact; the procedure is very similar to the one we are familiar with as 'praying'—requesting some discarnate or higher being to acknowledge its presence and waiting for a sign that the request has been received. This is also more or less the same procedure employed in casual sessions or séances of the curious: here the participants gathered request any entities present to indicate their replies by knocking, or answering questions by means of an Ouija board or planchette.

The difference is in the seriousness with which the experienced medium approaches his work. He has an appreciation of exactly what he is attempting to undertake and for that reason does not just ask 'whether anybody is there'. First he makes sure that he and any individuals he is dealing with, on both sides of the divide, are protected by invoking a higher power to request that his work be blessed. He expresses his sincere desire to learn and progress and asks for assistance to do so. Then he specifies the particular spirit or guide he wants to contact—and he must be prepared to wait in faith and trust for whatever answers he might be given. He also has to accept the fact that he might not receive an answer.

Working with his own familiar guides obviously streamlines the procedure, but no medium should ever lose sight of the seriousness of what he is doing.

I mentioned earlier that people often worry about whether they will encounter an 'evil spirit', though they have no real idea what an 'evil spirit' might be. I will repeat again, for this cannot be said enough times, that the serious student who carries out his work conscientiously, making sure he and his activities are protected through prayer, meditation and requests to be guided wisely, will almost never encounter any spirits or entities of an 'evil' nature. Psychic protection is most necessary, as we have seen, when the uninformed mess about with the spirit world in a casual way, for a thrill, 'a bit of fun' or out of simple ignorance. Sadly, ignorance is never any excuse if things go wrong, for the laws of the spirit world—like the physical world around us—apply whether the person who breaks them knows what he is doing or not.

In the physical world, we know that if you do not bother to lock your door but leave it open, the chances are that someone will walk into your house and help himself to your valuables. Whether you yourself are honest has nothing to do with it—you must take precautions against those who are not.

In the same way, people who casually open up the channels between this and the spirit world—inviting any spirits present to 'come through' with no idea of what might respond—are just asking for trouble. Irreverent séances or gatherings round the Ouija board (particularly if alcohol, which induces altered states of consciousness, is being consumed) are likely to have a similar effect to randomly posting your address on the Internet and announcing that the door is wide open and no-one is at home.

It is the lower order of spirits or entities, the bullying kind with little or no spiritual maturity which, as in this world, are most likely to respond (as in the case of the elemental I detailed earlier). In common with other practitioners, I have sometimes been called on to resolve the aftermath of cases where

110

'something', some entity or energy force has crashed through the barriers between the physical and the spiritual during such sessions. The results can be disturbance and distress, mental or physical illness—even, in a few grave cases, death.

With the balance of their mind disturbed by their experience, those involved can be driven to leap from windows, crash their cars or otherwise damage themselves or bring damage on others. There are innumerable horror stories of such incidents and the blame is usually placed on the Ouija board; in fact, like tarot cards, the board is just cardboard with no power of its own. The damage is done by the carelessness or stupidity of whoever might be using it.

When a person opens his or her mind willingly to some unspecified entity in spirit, they do not know what they might be letting loose and unfortunately such entities are difficult to deal with once they have been invited into someone's mind and space. The power of the will, highly respected by mediums, is often disregarded or misused by the 'ordinary' person.

Inspiration

'A poet is great, and is not a mere metrician, when he can discern and express emotive and spiritual ideas that lie hidden in the minds of men...
His art becomes almost a religion.'

Alfred Noyes
From a lecture on 'Poetry and Faith' given at Yale University

The fact that mental concentration and its application in a physical sense can produce immensely powerful results has been recognized throughout history; sheer survival often lay in out-witting a superior force using 'brain' rather than 'brawn' and applying the natural resources of the body. Breath is life-energy, and the effect is more powerful if sound is added and mantras used. Mantra means 'mind tool', and is the repeated chanting of a sacred name or phrase, which we see in Christianity—and other religions—reflected in the use of hymns and prayers, or by primitive tribes through ceremonial chanting.

When chanting, emotions are raised by means of the projected breath and directed by the willed use of sounds. Chanting changes the flow of oxygen to the brain, which can lead to altered states of consciousness—singing and speaking in a chanting way increases the oxygenation of the blood in a similar way to some yoga breathing exercises. We become 'inspired'.

But there are two meanings to the word 'inspiration'. We all inspire as we breathe air into our lungs—but we can also all be to whatever extent, the recipients as artists and mediums of some mysterious element referred to as 'inspiration' which links us with the deeper truths beyond normal consciousness. In spite of having made a spiritual commitment as a medium I live a material life every day. I breathe air to keep me alive, but my journey through this life also makes every breath a conscious connection with Spirit: for a dedicated artist, in the same way, the journey itself becomes the expression or translation of—a 'medium' for—whatever is granted intuitively.

'Air fills the space between earth and sky and in symbolic terms is linked with the wind, the breath and spirit. It is an invisible, animating force that links the individual with the cosmos and very often is the medium by which the gods communicate with humankind.'

Mark O'Connell and Raje Airey
Symbols, Signs & Visual Codes

However intense the mediumship might become, however aware of communion with spiritual dimensions, we are all of course human beings in physical form. Artists are notorious for trying to combine artistic inspiration with everyday drudgery by blurring the barriers between using drink or drugs. Some mediums—particularly if drawn to the shamanic tradition of working—do the same, altering their states of consciousness with drugs and/or using other methods like drumming or wild dancing to facilitate their entry into trance and enable communication to be made.

The early Norse warriors who were followers of Odin were known for their terrifying ability to enter a state of manic savagery known as 'going berserk' through such means—they were actually referred to as 'Berserkers'. And in ritual preparation before they fought, the Celts too painted themselves with dye and bleached their hair so that it stood thickly out from their heads: they went into battle naked, attacking their foes with such frenzy (called 'furor') that no-one could stand against them. There are similar accounts in most cultures of bands of warriors or other dedicated groups working themselves up through rituals of this nature, achieving a mindlessness that leaves their physical bodies open to whatever power they are trying to invoke. Unless controlled, such power can produce devastating violence and destruction—modern-day football crowds are examples of how groups can run wild with no awareness of the consequences.

These are the physical forces employed by a working medium in order to allow mental access to other states of being and consciousness, other worlds and dimensions. The build-up of the energies themselves are, like all such energies, neither good nor bad. Like water behind a dam they are there to be used, and this is why it so important for the medium or the artist to learn self-control. The medium especially is very aware of his role as a 'channel' for immense powers: intensive work on a high spiritual level can in extreme cases create such states of dissociation that the person may become 'mad'; even at much lower levels one can be left completely exhausted, physically and mentally vulnerable.

The daily training of a musician or dancer is a more familiar example of how forms of ritual can enable the body to transcend itself. The dancer Michael Flatley, for example, is on record as applying himself to his art in a remarkably similar way to the ancient Celtic warriors who provide his inspiration. Fitness trainer Pat Henry, who trained many actors and athletes at his gym in Dublin, described in 2004 how when he trained Michael for his show *Lord of the Dance* the performer's intense determination and focus was total— *'He is total concentration...'*

He noted the build-up of such power that one could almost see the results happening— *'when someone is that focused with that much meditation it happens. People were crying when he was dancing, bursting into tears with the feeling that they get from him dancing, because he's become meditation in action....*

'When you train somebody and they can meditate to that level, it can be scary,' he adds of such performers. *'People who meditate don't have any fear. There's no such thing as 'not going to be able to do this'. If you're in the presence of these guys before they go on stage they become tigers. They're no longer there at all. They are in their own 'other' space. They are in this meditation, and they move into that, and nobody and nothing can stop them. They're superhuman because they live in a different world...*

'When Michael first danced in his own show he became who he was meant to be, and I think that's the secret—become who you are meant to be.

'It all sounds rather strange but it's like a presence of God in a moving form. That's what it was. He wasn't there. It wasn't Michael Flatley, it was this movement that was flying through the air.'

116

At this level of commitment—whether artist or medium—one's whole life becomes a ritual of dedication and the results can be controlled and used for a positive or a negative outcome. It is often difficult to differentiate between them, for as I found during my historical research, humanity has a fascination with extremes, with both saints and sinners, and a habit of encouraging what I call 'The Cult of the Merry Rogue'.

Folk heroes throughout history from Robin Hood to Billy the Kid were not only dubious role models but prime examples of how intense motivation can be put to negative use. Even King Arthur's knights, for example, Richard the Lionheart's warriors of the Crusades or any of the lords who marched at the head of their forces with flags flying and banners waving, would actually in reality have been far from the romantic, heroic characters popularly portrayed. As mythological archetypes, such figures can inspire us to extremes of courage, but these men were killers—often sociopaths—whose focus and concentration was entirely motivated by the most basic, brutal selfishness and greed.

Similar popular folk heroes are still with us today but now they are likely to be presented as 'virtual' Exterminator-figures, real-life crime lords or convicted criminals, sportsmen/ athletes who all in their way, have a similar self-fixated, single-minded narrowness of vision. The same images have always been there in mythology and archetype—the hierarchies of Roman and Greek gods or even Celtic legends, for instance, were populated by characters remarkably like all-powerful Mafia dons.

In early societies we have seen that such primitive power was necessary for survival—or in the case of the athletes of ancient Greece, simply for the honour of winning. But in a materially wealthy culture—the Ancient Roman Empire, for example—where the spiritual became so demeaned that anything and everything, including divinity, could be bought, the downfall of that society was inevitable.

The novice medium—or anyone travelling this dedicated path—needs to be aware of the paradox. If goodness or evil is a choice made, if anyone can take the dark or light path it means we ignore the baser nature of man at our peril. All human beings possess the same dual nature and we must accept that spirituality has to embrace the temptations as well as the aspirations that arise from the extremes within us. The power of the dark side is just as relevant as that of the light.

Hitler and the Nazis based their philosophies on mythology accessible to all—the Norse cult of Odin. Their single-mindedness and particularly the sheer focus of Hitler's energy created a force that remains enduringly fascinating because it transcended the sum of its parts. Like the incredible artistry of a musician or dancer, this seemed inspired in the sense of being super-human—almost divine—though the gods it celebrated were warped, darkly pitiless divinities. The forces that can be built up from inspired energy have to be harnessed and controlled by the maturity and wisdom that comes only from submission of our personal wants and desires to the greater truth of Spirit.

'You treat this art like a religion.'
Ballerina Maria Tallchief

'We may think of this card (The Emperor) as representing the principle of everlasting life, the breath that God breathed into the clay when he made man, the divine inspiration that causes some to rise above the rest...
although this may be the spirit that makes men and women leaders...
it is also the spirit that fills great artists, mystics and saints.
It is a source of energy and a source of power: it initiates action
and then keeps it in continuing motion.'

Brian Innes
The Tarot: How to Use and Interpret the Cards

Talking to the Dead

I am often asked: Doesn't it frighten you to talk to the dead? (or indeed, to any discarnate spirits from other realms). But for a medium, it should be no more frightening than talking to the living—one simply uses one's mind to exchange thoughts instead of one's physical voice.

Some enquirers worry whether trying to make contact will harm departed loved ones— the state of death being seen as essentially 'at rest' or 'at peace'. But death is not an end, an abrupt finish. The departed are still there in spirit, just as we remember them, proceeding with the next stage of their journey: they are no more harmed by contact properly carried out, than if we had phoned them on some highly-developed cosmic phone-line, or were chatting on a slightly wider 'web' than we normally use.

In addition, no spirit is forced to communicate, though in my experience some response is usually given. Often I have found that another presence will bring a message if the individual asked for cannot, for whatever reason, come in person. I have encountered various reasons for non-appearance: sometimes the spirit is still 'finding his or her feet' in the realms beyond, perhaps weakened by a long illness. Though I find contact can usually be made within a very short period of passing over, even within hours, there are some individuals who appear to be still 'in recovery' years later—though time does not exist on the 'other side'. But by following accepted procedures properly, no spirit living or dead will ever be harmed by contact.

7
THE NOVICE MEDIUM

Interview with Dilys Gater
2 A Medium's Workbook

'Do not believe a thing because you read it in a book!
Do not believe a thing because another has said so!
Find out the truth for yourself.'

Swami Vivekananda

I have found that though in this materialistic age they might not admit it, enquirers have deeply serious personal reasons for consulting a medium. They want reassurance that death is not some kind of full stop to a pointless exercise but a mark of progress, a rite of passage like birth and growth, something meaningful in a positive way. The medium/priestess at the shrine, the shaman who can give such reassurance—even the artist—has been with mankind since the beginning and it is our own time that is increasingly 'out of joint'.

The official stance now conditions us to regard death as the ultimate enemy, an extreme form of 'un-wellness' to be avoided at

122

all costs, the worst possible fate to befall any individual. Indeed, the advances of science seem to indicate man's objective should be to carry on living for ever in a physical body, however aged or patched up, but most people I encounter are not happy with this idea; they recognize the essential falsity of the concept, the balance of nature interfered with. Death is a part of life as real, as inevitable—and as potentially valuable to us—as birth and all the other significant markers with which we measure our progress on Earth. And human beings, intuitively aware that they must eventually pass on, have always been comforted to receive messages from those who have crossed the boundary into the unknown ahead of them.

How do you get messages from the dead?

This is the question a medium is asked most often, with variations like:
- *How does the message come—do you see it, sense it, hear it?*
- *Do you find the spirits come in groups?*
- *Have you ever been able to communicate with animals?*
- *Are spirits like ghosts?*
- *How can you talk to the dead if reincarnation happens and/or they have been reborn in another body?*
- *What is it like on the other side?*

- And perhaps the most deeply felt of all, the anxious queries of the bereaved that I hear so often: *Is he/she all right? Do they know I love them and miss them?*

As a medium whose work involves ministering to the living, I am able to reassure the grieving that their loved ones are always 'all right' and they are always aware of having been loved. Whatever their circumstances in life, however ill, estranged or fearful they might have been, most spirits seem to recognize once they have passed over that all is well, that their physical pain and suffering has ended and they are in the place where they belong.

I have NEVER encountered a spirit that felt it was somewhere strange or frightening, in the wrong world, or wanted to return (though some spirits can be held back in situations involving an intense sense of guilt, the violent grief of others or similar extremes of human emotion). Neither have I encountered a spirit who claimed it had died too soon or—in the cases I have dealt with of people who had been murdered—wanted revenge or reprisal on his/her murderer. Suicides are different, and will be discussed later.

Life is only important to the Living

Once the soul or spirit has passed over it

seems to be remarkably indifferent about physical existence; it is even likely to regard its own death, however painful or long-drawn-out, as something in the nature of a bad dream from which it has now awakened. There are exceptions of course: I have encountered spirits who continue to join in family celebrations, look forward enthusiastically to their own funerals, or are so devoted to places where they were very happy (or unhappy) that they hang about and will not leave. Sometimes if they were in a very close relationship they tell the bereaved they will wait for them before proceeding further—but this is usually for the sake of the one who has been left behind. No departed soul ever feels abandoned or alone unless he has somehow created this state himself.

There are sad cases of guilty spirits who are afraid of whatever divine justice they might receive for their crimes on Earth and try to pretend they have not died; in other instances the dead have passed over without realizing it and are confused because they think they are still alive. But on the whole, the dead recognize that the physical span they have just lived out in a material body was only incidental to a far wider, much bigger picture; they continue their journey of further development and progress in spirit with no sense of loss.

Emotions as we experience them are part of the human condition and only exist in the spirit world on the 'lower levels' closest to us. The more elevated and refined the soul, the less human emotion it is likely to feel. But the process of refinement and elevation (however it occurs) does not just happen: and I have encountered many cases where the departed showed deep emotion and caring for those left behind. Unfortunately, the opposite is also the case and in one exceptional instance a woman's father, who had been consistently cruel and abusive to her in life, came through when he passed over with a highly emotional—and uncharacteristic—outburst of regret for his bad behaviour and appeal for her sympathy. After a few moments while she tried to adjust to this unexpected turn of events, I was aware of several other spirits intervening in outrage and indignation. Some of her departed uncles and aunts, who had known her father, were disgusted at this callous attempt to prey on her need for the love he had always denied her.

'You know what he was like,' they told her—as, sadly, she did. The spirit of her father, cowardly and unrepentant as always, immediately left the scene and her departed relatives tried to comfort her by reassuring her of their own care and love 'from all of us here, and from Auntie Minnie'.

126

How is contact made?

We have seen that most often the medium makes contact via one (or more) consistent communicant, a 'Spirit Guide' (sometimes called a 'control') who acts as a go-between, passing the messages through from either side—though I have never had such a 'control' and work directly with individual spirits. When working on behalf of someone wanting to make contact with a particular person I 'call' the departed spirit by focusing my concentration—usually on the name of the person with whom I want to communicate— and requesting their presence. Mostly the spirit responds, or if it does not, another comes in its place. There is usually some response within a few seconds—though on occasion, if the answer is silence, it is my duty to interpret the message inherent in the spirit world's lack of communication.

Often the spirit will come of its own accord while I am conducting a consultation and may indicate it has something important to communicate to the person having the session—perhaps it has been waiting some time to find a suitable medium to pass on its message. There are some mediums who stop comparative strangers in the street or another public place and tell them that someone in the spirit world has something to say to them—but

127

when one works in a disciplined and structured way this should not happen. It is vital for novice mediums to learn to be able to shut down the channels of communication unless actually working. Otherwise the instrument is being abused and the medium is likely to suffer stress and exhaustion or 'burnout'.

What is it like on the Other Side?

This is the greatest mystery of all, since the only ones who really know the answer are the dead themselves, but in my experience the departed are unable to tell us much. There is plenty of information about, including the teachings of the world's religions, but nothing has ever been conclusively proved. Throughout history every culture—Roman, Greek, Norse, Celtic—every pagan or primitive tribe—has had its own version of what happens when people die, but who in the 21st century seriously anticipates physically climbing into a boat to be rowed across to the Underworld, or joining the heroes to feast on Valhalla?

Jean Ritchie's account of 300 people's Near Death Experiences (*Death's Door*, published in 1994) is just one of innumerable similar reports of a phenomenon recognized today even by those with no belief or interest in spiritual matters. Near Death Experiences (or NDEs), the nearest thing we have to reports from the dead themselves, have many characteristics in common: there is a sense that the individual passes through a long dark corridor or tunnel, eventually emerging into a beautiful place of brightness and light often described as open countryside, perhaps with lovely blue skies, green grass, unlimited freedom. There seems a warm and all-pervading feeling of unconditional love, sometimes emanating from a mysterious, shining figure identified as God- or Christ-like; family members who have previously passed on may be gathered, smiling a welcome.

But once the physical body is dead, how can it be possible to live in any way remotely resembling the way we do now? And would we want to? A medium commented to me: 'The idea of spending eternity in any of the ways most people think we will—studying, learning new skills, even joining in harp-playing and singing, in a world that's just like this one only better—would bore me silly.'

My experience as a medium indicates that there are two aspects to the process of dying. First that much of the detail about the nature of 'heavens', 'hells' or any of the other places beyond this one is likely to be subjective in nature and based on the expectations of the individual—in the same way as 'Spirit Guides' always appear in whatever form is most appropriate and suited to the needs of that person.

Spirit provides us at every stage with what we can relate to best in our learning process, and there is probably a great deal of truth in the theory that we create our realities (including the realities we will encounter after death) ourselves. This would explain why so many of the dying react in a positive manner to what they perceive around them as they pass over. Many are filled with joy to see their departed partners, loved ones or relatives coming to fetch them and have a wonderful sense of 'going home'—which is exactly what happens to them.

On another level beyond the individual experience, however, there is the much wider picture of the soul's cosmic and on-going journey as it progresses to its ultimate end, union with the Source, the Divine. Commentators on both sides of the life/death divide have made various attempts to describe what this procedure might be like but again, as with all such matters, these will be utterly real to those who believe in them and meaningless to those who do not.

Many mediums, as well as 'ordinary' people have published accounts of what their 'Spirit Guides' or departed loved ones have told them about the world beyond—that there are universities of the mind, wonderful colours and light, parliaments of spirits and teachers whose mission is to help humanity learn and progress, graded Heavens up to the Seventh, through which the soul passes. (More information on all these and other concepts can be found in the writings of the 'Sleeping Prophet' Edgar Cayce; the writings of Frederick W. H. Myers, one of the founders of the Society for Psychical Research and author of *Human Personality and Its Survival of Bodily Death*; or via the SPR itself, the Theosophical Society or enquiring at any Spiritualist Church.)

Large numbers of individual books have also been published giving various accounts of 'what it is like' in the afterlife or what happens when we die. But my feeling is that these again are often extremely subjective. After a great deal of experience working with so-called ghosts still lingering here on Earth, with departed spirits and other disembodied entities from 'beyond the Veil' and with my own guides, I have learned to accept whatever comes through to me from Spirit without querying or trying to make sense of it—asking questions, for instance, like 'How could someone communicate if they have reincarnated in another body?' or 'If a person is still on Earth in ghostly form, how can they be on the other side as well?'; 'When does the soul enter or re-enter a physical body before a baby is born?' or 'Where is the soul if the person is in a coma or being kept alive by machinery?'

131

I have already mentioned that the processes of spiritual work are known as the Mysteries, and there is a great deal we are not expected to know or understand. The more I learn and progress, the more I realize how inadequate and limited my capabilities are. Primitive peoples were often too intuitively wise to bother about the practicalities we agonize over so much. They did not ask for answers. They did not ask for everything to be spelled out. They called their divine being—whatever it was—simply 'You', or 'The Nameless One' and did not question the guidance they received or where it was coming from. I have found that the closer one works with the Mysteries and with Spirit, the more one learns to query nothing except oneself.

The intuitive wisdom of the creative artist, the visions of poets, mystics, geniuses and even those regarded as mad, may be far more accurate than any dogmatic teaching about the nature of other dimensions. Helen Wambach's book *Life Before Life* recounted the experience of volunteers who regressed to the pre-birth and birth state and discovered among other things that: *'In the world between lifetimes, our chronological time system and whether one is physically alive or dead seem of relatively little importance.'* Many reported a sense of omnipotent knowledge as a baby, a feeling

132

that those in the world (ie: adults on the Earth, into which the baby had just been born) were actually the ignorant ones.

This is something often expressed by great artists and even 'ordinary' people—that we are born with intuitive awareness of the Mysteries with which we lose touch as we grow. The poet Wordsworth is only one who has put this feeling into words, writing in his *Ode on the Intimations of Immortality from Recollections of Early Childhood:*

Our birth is but a sleep and a forgetting:
The Soul that rises with us, our life's Star,
Hath had elsewhere its setting,
And cometh from afar:
Not in entire forgetfulness,
And not in utter nakedness,
But trailing clouds of glory do we come
From God who is our home:
Heaven lies about us in our infancy!
Shades of the prison-house begin to close
Upon the growing Boy,
But He beholds the light, and whence it flows,
He sees it in his joy;
The Youth, who daily farther from the east
Must travel, still is Nature's Priest,
And by the vision splendid
Is on his way attended;
At length the Man perceives it die away,
And fade into the light of common day.

How do I get the messages?

My work over the last six years has included two books of sustained trance mediumship which will be discussed later. This was something new and exciting, for most of the time I am not 'clairaudient'. I do not 'hear voices' except on rare occasions when I will get specific words or phrases; most of the communications I receive—whether 'channelled' or speaking to a departed spirit—pass into my mind as knowledge or awareness I then have to translate into words. The process, expressed by many mediums and intuitive artists, is similar to 'tuning in' to radio signals that may sometimes be very faint and sometimes very clear—the choreographer Sir Frederick Ashton, for example, used these words when describing how he received inspiration for his ballets:

'I rather put myself in the hands of a superior power. I make some kind of receptive preparation. I am almost like a wireless. I feel that if I turn the right knobs the stream will flow through me.'

I also find the metaphor of trying to read the 'dots and dashes' of Braille or Morse, or receiving a signal in code via a different sense to the ones I usually use, helps to describe the process. More details are given in a later chapter.

134

In cases where 'channelled' material passes through my mind there is no sense of lettering or punctuation, only the meaning itself. When I write the words down I add the minimum necessary in the form of full stops, commas and capital letters to break up the continuous flow into sentences that will make it coherent to a reader.

Communicating with animals

I have communicated with departed animals many times, and find in general that they do not give messages in words but in images or as feelings—though on one occasion a pet dog who had passed over proved to be a highly developed spirit which had advanced philosophical and metaphysical teachings to impart to its grieving owner. The earliest animal messages I received were from a deeply missed Cornish Rex cat, which revealed it was in a lovely garden and brought the image of a large yellow sunflower; and a white horse that had belonged to an Afghan nobleman I knew in London, which 'wanted to be remembered' to him.

As a medium I have seen departed pets reunited with owners who have passed over themselves; I have encountered departed pets who have companion animals with them in the spirit world; and one departed dog who had angelic links. It appears too that though

I do not have a 'control' when dealing with departed people, I have been granted one when working with departed animals. On one occasion the dog (a spaniel) who had passed did not come herself, but a black and white mongrel which I could only describe as extremely 'street-wise' nonchalantly appeared to explain that she was resting but sent loving thoughts. This was the first occasion that the 'go-between'—an animal version of a 'spirit guide' or 'control'—most unexpectedly appeared, and I have encountered this very individual character several times since.

The Chariot

The impetus of the Chariot card in the tarot pack signifies that it is up to each individual to grasp gifts and opportunities bestowed, but also to be aware that there are limitations to what can be achieved by a physical being. Sometimes we can be swept into deeper waters than we can cope with, and it may be more prudent to query our own abilities rather than to regard ourselves as infallible.

The Chariot also warns us to conserve our powers. One of the rules governing psychic work and mediumship is that you cannot exist in several different dimensions at the same time. You have to move between them and the effort can be detrimental to both physical and mental health. We have seen how creative artists can ruin their health pursuing their vision and that it is the same for a medium, treading a fine line between visionary mysticism and madness.

The medium Pamela Ball has made the comment that: *'Clairvoyant flashes can seriously disturb the equilibrium and have considerable emotional impact.'*

This is true, especially for the inexperienced. Both the medium and the artist are on dangerous ground, venturing into territories where the human foot cannot rightfully tread. Their work involves defining the nature of the boundary between living and dying—exploring the threshold—and we have seen that incredible amounts of energy are used when opening the channels for communication between different worlds or dimensions. Input is necessary from all sides since—so far as we can tell—it often takes as great an effort for spirits of whatever level to make contact with us as it does for us to reach them.

The medium must conserve his strength. You can lose touch with everyday reality by wanting to rush in too fast or by abandoning the basic disciplines as boring and long-drawn-out, especially if you have reached a 'plateau' state where little appears to be happening. The Chariot reminds us to step cautiously: that power does not necessarily bring enlightenment with it.

137

'Just as the conqueror stands self-assured and
self-confident in his chariot,
so at this level man also acquires these
characteristics. He begins to know
his own powers, but he has already reached the
stage where he knows, and does not forget, that
all these powers are not his but belong to God.
He now knows that without God he is nothing,
that he receives
all his abilities and talents from the single primal
source of all powers.'

Elisabeth Haich (Translated by D Q
Stephenson)
The Wisdom of the Tarot

The Call to Serve

There are no such things as 'amateur'
mediums. Everyone aspiring to mediumship
should take his work very seriously, for if
one has the gift it is something very real and
potentially extremely powerful. In *Urban
Shaman* I quoted a native Indian shaman's
description of himself as 'apprenticed to the
gods': in a similar way the medium is privileged
to be 'apprenticed to Spirit'.

For the Celts, power was domination in
the most physical sense. Loss of a loved one
could even provoke the desire to absorb the

corpse physically into oneself, as described in *Eimher's Keen over Chu Chulainn*, penned by an unknown Irish writer in the 15th century and translated by Kenneth Hurlstone Jackson in *A Celtic Miscellany*. Here the beheaded hero is mourned by his wife:

'Then Cenn Berraide arose and brought the head to Dun Delgan, and gave it into Eimher's hand; and she had it washed and put it on its own body, and Eimher took it to her, and she clutched it to her breast and her bosom after that, and began to bewail and lament over him, and began to kiss his lips and drink his blood, and she put a silken shroud about him.'

It is this intense physicality, the willingness to sacrifice everything—one's life if necessary—that marks the dedication with which those chosen by Spirit must pledge themselves. Only when they have relinquished all physical power of their own are they granted the mental and spiritual empowerment to go forward along the way marked out for them.

As my own gifts developed I found them very difficult to accept—any 'ordinary' person feels the same. It was very much a question of: 'Why me? Why now?' So for others who have difficulty in believing they may have been singled out to fulfill a spiritual calling, here is the answer that was given to me: 'Somebody has to do it—so why *not* you? And why *not* now?'

139

PART THREE
THE MOONLIT DOOR

'Is there anybody there?' said the Traveller
Knocking on the moonlit door

'I do not deny that communication with the Spirit World is full of perplexities. Answers to questions put to spirits are often contradictory and apparently misleading.

'Generally, this is owing to the difficulty experienced in describing to beings who are functioning in three dimensions what is taking place in a region inhabited by those who are functioning in four or more.'

William Usborne Moore, a retired vice-admiral turned psychic investigator, wrote this in 1911 in his *Glimpses of the Next State*.

'I never said that it was possible…I only said that it was true.'
Sir William Crookes
(on the psychic phenomena he observed and reported as a scientist)

140

*'I never came upon any of my discoveries
through the process of rational thinking.'*
Albert Einstein

Across the Divide

We have seen how mythology and folk
tradition often views the life/death
boundary—the place of crossing—as a river,
a continuously flowing elemental barrier
that bars those on each side from venturing
into the realms of the other. The medium
stands on one bank, as it were, and receives
communications from the 'other side' which
can then be passed on to the recipient/s.

But communication is not a simple matter.
One of the reasons why prophets, seers and
oracles tend to speak in a 'language' of their
own, why a clairvoyant ('one who sees clearly')
or a medium ('a way', 'path' or 'channel') can
sound vague is because they have to express
concepts and truths from other worlds less
finite than this, in language which is inevitably
finite. Definitions restrict, whereas what
psychics and mediums deal with is a removal
of barriers and boundaries. The ideal form
of communication would be made instantly,
thought transferred from one mind or spirit to
another: that way there is no barrier, no need
for interpretation; no need to query whether
what was communicated was true, because

141

there is no way it could be false.

I have mentioned that enormous amounts of effort can be necessary to make contact from this side—that members of closed Circles contribute their energies to assist the medium in his or her work. But the communicating spirit of Professor Frederick Myers reveals that it is just as frustrating when trying to make contact from the other side:

'The nearest simile I can find to express the difficulty of sending a message—is that I appear to be standing behind a sheet of frosted glass which blurs sight and deadens sound—dictating feebly to a reluctant and somewhat obtuse secretary.'

8
THE PLACE BETWEEN

'Is there anybody there?' said the Traveller
 Knocking on the moonlit door;
And his horse in the silence champ'd the grasses
 Of the forest's ferney floor:
And a bird flew out of the turret
 Above the Traveller's head
And he smote upon the door again a second time:
 'Is there anybody there?' he said.

Walter de la Mare
The Listeners

When we make contact with the 'other side' we are, to whatever degree, suspending disbelief; we enter voluntarily into a mental state that has been described as 'when the clock strikes thirteen', 'a gap in time', 'between the past and future'. Mystics and visionaries know this state, artists are familiar with it and the best-known poem in the English language, Walter de la Mare's *The Listeners* describes it so very well. Perhaps this is why the poem makes such an impact.

The mysterious Traveller arriving at a meeting place, knocking on the moonlit door to be met by silence and 'a host of phantom listeners' is perhaps the most recognizable descriptive image there is of a medium's work; *Psychic News* (December 13, 2008) reported the guest appearance of Judith Seaman, Vice-President of the Spiritualists' National Union's on BBC4's *Adventures in Poetry* programme where the work under discussion was this same poem.

'*The opening line... is traditionally what people think of as the introduction to a Spiritualist séance, when people come together to try to communicate with the Spirit World,*' Mrs Seaman explained. '*Knocking—rapping—was the earliest form of communication recognized in modern Spiritualism....So the opening line is inferring towards... someone searching for a personal communication with discarnate beings.*' She added that the SNU's course *Mediumship in Art and Science* also examines—as indeed does this book—'*the inspirational effects of spirit on writers, painters, musicians and scientists.*'

The Listeners wonderfully encapsulates the airy spaces inhabited by initiates of the Mysteries. Neither the Traveller's errand nor his identity is explained; we do not know what the building in the forest is nor who are the listeners within—and most of all, why they do not answer. When asked by the presenter 'to comment on the unanswered knock', Mrs Seaman gave the 'official' Spiritualist explanation that: *'Many people come to a medium in search of personal communication, but it's necessary to remember that the communication is initiated from the Spirit World. They make the initial contact, and perhaps it's reflected in the poem that it's not possible for us to call up the 'dead'. It isn't, but certainly the discarnate can communicate with us if they choose to do so.'*

My own experience as a 'maverick' medium working with Spirit is that contact can just as easily be made from either side. But however contact is made I find the image of the Moonlit Door doubly relevant, even crucial.

'I see it as it is in the poem,' I wrote in my early notes for this book, 'the shadowed wooden door of some unknown dwelling in the forest, a heavy door, with an ancient iron latch, tightly shut, with shutters on the windows and a looming, heavily gabled roof above. We cannot see inside, and we hesitate before we knock, wondering whether anyone will answer—half-afraid of what might happen if they do.'

Like the ancient temples of the Oracle, the 'Moonlit Door' marks the place between the worlds of the living and the dead where the priestess/medium officiates, whether knocking

145

upon the 'Moonlit Door' or sitting in trance in the inner room of the shrine above the fissure in the rock or sacred spring. It is a mystical place removed from time and space. There is a sense of incense, smoke, visions induced by the drug, transcendent awareness.

'...air was often thought to be a fine material intermediary realm between the earthly and spiritual realms; it was sometimes seen as a symbol of spirit, which is invisible to the eye, yet noticeable in its effects.'

Udo Becker (Translated by Lance W. Garmer)
The Continuum Encyclopedia of Symbols

*   *   *

Since all activities are carried out in the mind, in a space of mental focus and concentration, each medium's view of the life/death boundary and their way of working will be different. But generally the medium does not cross the boundary himself: either a 'Spirit Guide' acts as intermediary, bringing souls which want to communicate to the boundary or (as in my case) the individual spirit/s come to the boundary on their own. The medium does not usually venture into the world of the dead or any other world—such journeys are of a different kind.

The image of the Moonlit Door is a poetic

vision of the medium's work but regarding the mechanics—the 'nuts and bolts' of the exchange, how it is carried out— other pictorial concepts can also help to make the procedure comprehensible. I view the boundary between life and death as similar to the border between different countries; people cross by the 'main route out' when their time comes and do not return in a physical sense as physical return is not possible—some spirits have even jokingly pointed out to me that they no longer have a body, though they are far from 'dead'. After years of experience in mediumship however, I found that for me, in practical terms, there is no single boundary or barrier at the place of crossing between life and death. Instead there are several parallel boundaries enclosing a kind of 'no man's land' or common territory between the worlds of the living and the dead.

Contact seems most usually to be made in this neutral zone which is neither life nor death but something that lies between them. I think of this place as 'the anteroom' and imagine it as similar to the 'airlocks' or decompression chambers in accounts of space flight or descent into the ocean depths. Imagine that the dead can enter this 'anteroom' from their world by a sort of revolving door, and I am able to enter at this side from mine, and so we can meet and communicate in comfort.

147

The Anteroom

The 'anteroom' has over the years become increasingly relevant and important in my experience of communication with the spirits and the dead. I do not know whether a concept such as an 'anteroom' exists in any formal religious teaching, but I have not come across one that seems right to me. The accepted view of a purgatory, which seems to be the nearest in a theological sense, is defined in the Mini Oxford Dictionary as 'a condition, place of spiritual purging... of souls departing this life in the grace of God but requiring to be cleansed from venial sins, etc.,' 'a place of temporary suffering or expiation'. The verb 'to purge' has quite a violent connotation, indicating drastic cleansing or purifying, 'making physically or spiritually clean' on every level.

I have no sense of this kind of 'purging' or even of suffering, and in most cases find the souls which have passed are 'in recovery' after the traumas of living and dying. The existence of this kind of 'buffer zone' makes particular sense as it can take various forms, as required. Often I find it appears as a 'recovery room' if a person has died after a long period of pain and debilitation—they have 'crossed' safely and are now gathering strength before they are ready to proceed further, as it were. The 'recovery room' sometimes presents itself almost like an extension off the hospital ward or operating theatre where the patient died; sometimes it can take the form of a room in a beautiful country house where they have been taken to 'recuperate; often there is just a sunlit garden or green countryside and open space.

But whatever the setting, and though there may be other spirits present, I am always aware that this is not the eventual destination but a 'halfway house', a plain, utilitarian space allowing communication to take place across an unbridgeable divide—another image I find applicable here would be the 'parlour' or 'turn' in a convent. The word 'parlour' comes from a root that means 'a place to talk': when I hear of other mediums communicating with the departed by means of spirit guides who 'bring across' those who have something to say, I imagine such guides probably inhabit similar 'anterooms' into which they admit each individual spirit in turn. Spiritualist belief regards the world beyond this as the 'Summerland', a similar place to the Christian Heaven—but my experience is as described, of a neutral zone, a 'staging post' rather than any actual destination.

I personally can view this space and enter it but in most exchanges am not permitted to go further. So when communicating in this way I can conduct a conversation with whatever spirit/s might be present but am not permitted to follow it/them out on the other side and into

149

the realms of the departed myself. Similarly, when carrying out past life regressions or other work where I have 'seen' a former death, I can accompany those concerned up to the point of death but not go further with them. I have described what happens as 'just a blank, as though the film spun off the reel. You were gone'. I know intuitively that I must not 'cross the boundary' with a person who dies but must wait until the time comes for me to cross myself.

But I do get glimpses or awareness of life beyond death in other ways less easy to describe. It is as though I cannot follow the departed person via the usual path through the 'antechamber' and across the divide, but using a different process can sidetrack and cross at a different point. My image for this is like crossing a border avoiding guarded checkpoints and border patrols on the main roads, and taking instead a little-known unguarded path into the forbidden country. In this way it is possible to 'cross over' at some distance from the main route and return the same way.

The Second Death

Though I have read and studied a great deal about the subject of death, I have not encountered any generally accepted explanation accounting for the 'neutral

150

zone' or 'antechamber'. It may well exist somewhere—the nearest are perhaps the Spiritualist 'Summerland' or the Tibetan 'between' state called *'bardo'*—and following on this comes another state, that of the 'Second Death'.

Michael E. Tymn (author of *Running on Third Wind* and *The Articulate Dead*) has described a condition called 'the Second Death' in these words: *'...immediately after the silver cord breaks and the physical body releases the spiritual, ie. 'gives up the ghost', there is some stress, some confusion, some struggling in the spirit person's attempt to adjust to his or her new condition. When the adjustment is made, the second death is experienced.'*

He cites repeated use of the term 'the second death' in the Book of Revelations, and explores various theories of how *'the second death takes place within hours or a few days for the spiritually advanced, but may take months or years in earth time for the spiritually challenged, those who remain earth-bound.*

'In effect,' he points out, *'the second death is an awakening to one's condition based on one's spiritual consciousness in the earth life.'*

The interim between physical and 'second death' might thus be regarded as another form of life, lived in a different body which also has to be shed before the freed spirit eventually passes completely. This 'transition stage' is described by Tymn as:

151

'..an intermediate or staging area of sorts where the soul must adjust...to the Spirit World'. He points out that according to the New Testament, Jesus chose to spend several days in this state before 'ascending into Heaven' on the third day after his bodily death.

In this case the airy 'place between' that bridges the earthly and truly spiritual realms— whatever it is that lies at the 'crossing place' between the moment of physical death and the occurrence of the 'second death', with its irrevocable acceptance of purely spiritual existence—is in itself a realm of existence. My own experience, as I have said, indicates that this is largely where most communications by mediums are made, and that even though some contacts may be from further (or 'higher') realms, these are very difficult for a human brain to understand or express.

The teachings of White Eagle via medium Grace Cooke also explore the concept of the 'Second Death', expressing many of the points made above. *'Man brings about his own death, by his ignorance, by the unconscious breaking of divine law...There may be a change of form, but we do not use the word 'decay'... When ignorance is replaced by knowledge, the body will be retained as long as it is needed; there will come instead a quickening of the vibrations of the physical atoms, which will lead*

152

to the transition of the body to a higher plane of activity...

'Armageddon does not take place in a great earthly battle, but within man's own heart, in the battle between his spirit and his lower self,' White Eagle explains. *'...People are mistaken when they think of the world of spirit as being something outside, something beyond this present life. We all talk about a life beyond; we use certain words loosely and thereby convey the wrong meaning...The physical plane, the astral, the etheric, the mental, the celestial—all these planes inter-penetrate. You cannot yet fully understand what this means, you are limited by a mental conception as to the nature of space and time...'*

Similar 'technical' details found in many other teachings appear to agree that the 'next world' or even the 'underworld referred to as Hell or Hades' are largely states of confusion created by man in his mistaken fixation with the purely material aspects of living. Those spiritually prepared will pass through quickly and easily—or even by-pass the state altogether—and continue their journey of development with no delay. Others, as discussed later, may need to 'work through' their awareness and appreciation of the spiritual before they can move on.

The Interpreter

Early in my psychic career I was advised from various sources that it was my job to be 'an interpreter'. This makes a lot of sense, for I found that a great deal of my work as a medium was to involve sifting through messages or 'channelled' material that had to be 'translated' into a coherent form. Some mediums 'hear' sentences and words clearly, as though their communicant is speaking to them and they simply relay the message in a phonetic kind of way—even, on occasion, being able to 'receive' or 'channel' material in a different language, possibly one they cannot speak themselves.

I have explained that sometimes I get actual words, but mainly the 'messages' I receive seem to come through in various forms of code similar to Morse, Braille or complicated data on a computer print-out. During my work of sustained trance mediumship over the last half-dozen years, however, I carried out sessions where words, impressions and various other forms of communication were all used.

'I work as a 'code-breaker',' I wrote during these years, 'a translator into understandable form of information that comes encrypted, and is not what it appears on the surface. The image I have of myself at this point is similar to those war-time pictures that so thrill us in

154

nostalgia movies—the code-breaker sitting at a desk, huddled over a machine (called, of course 'Enigma') in the light of a green-shaded lamp, noting down dots and dashes, letters and numbers, forming long columns of words. The code-book lying on the desk is torn and tattered, possibly out of date. The code-breaker is trying his utmost to use his experience and ingenuity to affect a breakthrough. Communication must be made. The message must get through safely. Lives could depend on the outcome'.

One of the most difficult obstacles for mediums to overcome is their very humanity. However dedicated or genuine, they are fallible beings: the machine is not perfect. No messages of any kind from the Beyond can be accepted as proven fact, though believers in formal religion are inclined to treat their holy texts in this way. In a Spiritualist sense there are some wonderfully consistent texts available in the public domain from elevated guides like Silver Birch and White Eagle, but since there is no way to 'grade' or license mediums as to the quality of their work or actual ability, there are also large numbers of less than adequate products of mediumship about.

Many beginners and even some more advanced practitioners lack the ability to continually scrutinize themselves and their mediumship in order to progress. Often I have heard the bereaved wanting messages from their loved ones being given simply unconditional reassurances of sweetness and love. It seems to be accepted that this is how it is on the other side, that everyone is bathed in a rosy glow which rubs out any negative aspect of existence or thought—or personality.

This kind of universal sentiment is all some people are able to take, and one could carry on at this level for years—indeed, many mediums appear to do so. Creative artists too, may not possess the desire or the ability to progress further than this comfortable state which offers nothing challenging to the medium, the artist or any recipients of their work. But as the medium develops, he should become aware that contrary to the well-meaning but excessive sentimentality often prevailing in groups or con-gregations, many departed spirits remain 'sinners' rather than 'saints', with all the 'bad habits' they might have had when alive. Crossing over does not automatically rub out the darker aspects of existence, in whatever form the spirit may now dwell, and the developing medium must learn to differentiate between the subtle layers of meaning in any communications he receives.

For example, it is believed by some that every single message of any kind received from the Beyond is completely and utterly true. Messages from Spirit itself are always expressions of Divine truth, since they cannot be otherwise, but experience teaches the medium that departed spirits do not necessarily tell the truth, for all kinds of reasons. He must learn to trust his spiritual intuition and guidance rather than accept words or messages at their face value sometimes. Like the abusive father I encountered who tried to con his daughter to gain her sympathy, the dead will continue to use whatever strategies they habitually used when alive; more times than one might imagine, messages from departed souls are deliberately inaccurate, even downright untrue, reflecting the efforts that person would have made in life to 'keep up appearances'.

When I was working in trance with the English Romantic composer Sir Arnold Bax on our book *Summer with Bax*, I picked up that he had suffered from chest or throat weakness when alive, and said so. Immediately his response came back:

'I was disgustingly healthy,' he declared.

But my husband Paul's research revealed Bax had in fact suffered from a heart murmur all his life (at one stage, a doctor even told his parents he was suffering from acute heart disease with only weeks to live). Characteristically though, he would not admit to a less than perfect physique even after he had departed his body.

I have rarely—if ever—encountered a departed spirit which communicated entirely in saintly and flowery speeches full of sweetness, light and peace and would regard such a communication as probably a cover-up for something else. What makes the exchanges real for me is the unexpectedness of what comes through even in expressions of love— or the lack of love sometimes. The spirits communicating, like the mediums, can remain very human indeed.

So uncritical acceptance is not necessarily always the best attitude, especially if the novice wishes to develop and progress. There are innumerable aspects of communication to take into account—for instance, books, texts and messages (especially if received from a departed relative or much-loved family member) may well be biased: the bereaved want to perpetuate their loving memories and are reluctant to think ill of the dead. The ability of each 'Interpreter' to translate whatever he receives into words and images the reader can understand should also be considered.

Some critics find fault with mediums because the language of messages may be very limited vocabulary-wise, or express itself in sentimental and untutored phraseology. I was inclined to think like this myself when considering some of the work of other mediums, until I realized that the medium is his own instrument, and the limitations of his brain will be reflected in his 'translations' of what he is given from those in spirit. Not every medium is able to be clinically detached or capable of clear, literate prose. Each does the best he can.

This is also why many texts supposedly from the beyond read like Victorian sermons or use Biblical language. They are what the medium himself, perhaps brought up as I was, familiar with Sunday School and traditional Church or Chapel services, would expect to hear or read.

Sending the spirit home

When communication in the 'anteroom' is over I mentally make sure the spirit returns to where it belongs. I do not know what other mediums call this but I refer to it as 'seeing the spirit home' or 'clearing the channel'. Over the years I learned that this is just as necessary as opening up the channels of communication, particularly since some spirits want to stay and 'chat' or are reluctant to return to their own realm. As I have mentioned, the medium must always act responsibly towards both the enquirer and any spirit summoned to answer the enquiry.

The procedure of ensuring the spirit makes a safe return happens once again in the mind for me, through focusing my concentration in one of several ways:

- I can watch it cross a flowery meadow until it reaches the boundary on the far side or goes out of my sight.
- I can watch it climb a rocky path up the side of a high mountain until it has disappeared over the summit and gone out of my view.

These two are the most usual departure scenarios, but sometimes the spirit has a more personal method of 'returning home'. I watched one man mount his old-fashioned touring bicycle and cycle off round the edge of a beautiful lake into the far distance; another woman simply stepped through a door into a walled garden. Mostly the spirit comes and returns alone, but there are occasional variations. It may be accompanied by a departed pet, with which it has been united. And in my work there is sometimes an awareness of the presence of other spirits, but they rarely participate.

Loving thoughts and prayers on behalf of the dead from those who have been left behind may have a far deeper significance than we commonly imagine. Apart from being a comfort to the bereaved, all my experience as a medium reinforces the idea outlined above that the dead are undertaking their own

160

further progress in spirit and need helpful energy and encouragement from the living. They have to learn when they pass into a more spiritual existence, to refine their awareness and work on their personal perceptions and values. So loving interaction reflects how communication with the dead—just like communication with the living—is very much a two-way affair with need for support on both sides.

Though it is popularly believed that mediums contact the departed to hear 'what the future holds', the dead appear to have little more knowledge about the future than we do: some accounts of their recorded pronouncements reveal themselves on examination to be largely wishful thinking. (Prophetic suggestions over the last hundred years or so that the world is about to enter a beatific phase of universal understanding, peace and love, for example, seem to me to fall very much into this category.)

On many occasions I have found it realistically reassuring when spirits who have been consulted—usually about what course of action the enquirer should take—have admitted they don't know the answer. Some mothers remind their daughters: 'You are older now than I was when I had you', sometimes even: 'You are older now than I was when I died!'

Age does not necessarily bring wisdom,

161

though it is a common human delusion that our parents 'knew better' than their children. And neither, it appears, does death bestow sudden and infinite knowledge. The message I usually find I am passing on in such cases is that the spirits trust those they have left behind to discover their own strength within themselves and act wisely. They tell the bereaved how proud they are of them, how they have every confidence in their ability to cope.

It appears too that living individuals cannot choose whether or not they will be able to send specific messages back to those who survive them when they have passed on. Instances of people telling their loved ones that they will communicate with them when they die— sometimes even agreeing on a cryptic sentence or codeword which will prove they have survived—have rarely produced results. So far as I am aware, it is not possible to do this. You cannot bypass the actual barrier between life and death and make cold-blooded plans to suit yourself.

Please give me some message of
encouragement.
I'm trying to shine.

Beyond the pen and the head is the open space
where you must dwell
to be free of confinement. Birth is a death &
death a birth. Your writing
is a passage to that birth—a long skein-sleeve to
be passed through.
A passage. Move on my darling, do not linger or
hesitate.
Pass on.

The Pupil
Conversations with Mist

'In her left hand (the High Priestess) holds two
keys. These are the keys to this world and the
next. She has access to both worlds, she can lock
or unlock the gates, enter or leave as she pleases.
But she does not divulge the mysteries of these
worlds to the immature.'

Elisabeth Haich (Translated by D Q
Stephenson)
The Wisdom of the Tarot

9
AT THE STILL POINT

I'm going round in circles—
That is as it should be.
Why?
The circle is eternal—it is all and yet nothing.
The Pupil
Conversations with Mist

*'The symbolic centre had great significance for
the Celts.'*
Stephen Allen
Lords of Battle: The World of the Celtic Warrior

The ancient Celts spoke languages largely
unknown today, though Gaelic and Welsh
have survived (albeit in modern forms). But
the Druids also communicated by other
means: they used the patterns of oral poetry;
Ogham, the language of the trees and the
mysterious symbolism of the Runes. In various
forms these can still be studied and the artist
or medium continue to be inspired by the
elements, the natural world, the traditions
of ancient elders and wise teachers of tribal
ancestry. Music and sound, sight, vision
and image have always played their part in
communication too, providing other forms

164

of language when words proved inadequate. In the same way that artists and poets are 'inspired' by visions they have difficulty in describing, much of the information received by a medium has to be presented in symbolic imagery in order to make it comprehensible to a recipient: at a much deeper level, communication is not just about the words or images themselves.

I mentioned earlier that as the medium (or artist) progresses in experience and maturity, he stops asking questions and simply follows the instruction of his guides, whether these are perceived as spiritual presences, muses or just vague 'inspiration'. The artist may unaccountably enter a 'blue period'; or discover some entirely new and original form of expression; the composer likewise, may suddenly begin to produce work that is unlike any he has produced before. We see this in the arts when a performer known in the area of popular music 'crosses over' and makes an appearance in the classics or vice versa. A comedian, say, undertakes a Shakespearean role—in recent times, Lenny Henry's performance of Othello, which I saw and admired, was a case in point.

When one has reached the threshold, the 'still point', the 'place between' one finds oneself communicating in different ways because here, everything changes. Moving forward or progressing in a chronological sense, stops. One may move in quite different directions—or may not even appear to move at all. But the 'still point' is not necessarily still. Whether perceived as the source of the Mysteries or simply the threshold of some mysterious goal we aspire to reach, this place is pivotal. It is where the focus changes.

The Wheel of Fortune

'This card heralds a fresh start. You are embarking on a new chapter and it is up to you to determine whether this will be a positive or negative experience. There may be a turn of events that you could not have predicted and over which you have no control, or an important decision to make...

'The Wheel of Fortune is reminding you that change is inevitable, for without it life would stagnate and you would cease to grow and develop your potential...'

Annie Lionnet
The Tarot Directory

In Celtic as well as many other belief systems the shape of a wheel or circle has hugely magical symbolism. It indicates a mystical path, incorporating as it does such images as the Celtic knot, the spiral, the labyrinth, which can be found everywhere in Wales. The 12th century Celtic font in St Beuno's Church, Pistyll for instance, is carved with a

166

design depicting life without beginning or end, only one of the many instances where pagan symbolism and belief was so strong it was incorporated into the Christianity brought to these pagan isles at a later date.

Other ancient concepts also view life and death not as states that progress from one to the other but as different points on a wheel— the Wheel of Life or Fortune. The image is the same whether of continuing reincarnation and rebirth; of the energy points of the body known as the chakras, spinning yet still; the prayer wheel; the Red Indian medicine wheel.

Essentially this is an image of time stilled, yet continuing to occur.

At the centre of the wheel is the 'still point' surrounded by movement; the eye of the storm, the 'place between' of balance, harmony and awareness. Both the Moonlit Door and the 'inner chamber' of ancient shrines mark this point, which remains unaffected by whatever storms, tempests or confusions may rage around it. In this 'place between' every aspect of the experience of life and death is encompassed. Opposite extremes touch and fuse. Death may be life and life death. The wheel continues to turn. There is no end to the circle, no place where life stops: and the centre is the pivot around which everything else revolves.

So if the vision and awareness is of life as a wheel that continues to revolve with no beginning and no end—not a strict progression through time from birth to death and beyond—the act of communication must also be perceived differently. It is not made chronologically backwards or forwards, simply from different points on the circle. The overall vision becomes a much wider one, and when working with Spirit—or even with 'inspiration', the enquirer learns that so far as communication by questions and answers are concerned, the entire concept changes.

Initially the novice medium is likely to visualize the procedure of communicating as described in *The Listeners*—one approaches the point of contact, the 'Moonlit Door' and knocks upon it to request answers. The novice learns that in most cases, communication will be made and answers given—though as William Usborne Moore points out, the answers may be difficult to comprehend or interpret. As the novice progresses, however, he learns that in the 'still place between' it is not necessary to ask questions at all, simply to accept what is given. Spirit provides all answers but they will not necessarily be in response to the enquirer's questions—especially as he may not even know what questions to ask.

The medium perceives that people communicating between worlds, too, are simply at different points on the circle. It is just the viewpoint which is different.

I began to wonder whether *The Listeners* held far more significance than being a wonderful description of the act of mediumship. The Traveller was not just an individual in this world, seeking answers from the 'other side' of the 'Moonlit Door'. If the 'Moonlit Door' marks the still point at the centre of the wheel of life/death, there can be no 'other side'. What if the door, situated at the central point of the wheel, is exactly the same door, approached from different points of the circle? What if, whichever place one knocks it is always 'this side' and there is no 'other side' at all?

In this (to me) revelatory as well as revolutionary context, there can be no difference between life, death, the 'anteroom' or any other state of being souls might inhabit; these states are only different points on the wheel. The reality is of travellers all progressing in their different ways, all knocking at their own version of the door trying to reach an 'other side' that does not exist. In this context, spirits might be knocking to make contact with us, under the impression that it is we who stand on the other side, not them.

We have reached the *'place which is beyond the physical, yet still with physical boundaries'*

169

which I described at the beginning of the book. Here at the hidden shrine or 'Moonlit Door', the artist or medium begins to communicate in other ways in order to explore the threshold on which he stands; his aim is now: *'...to discover how best to exist there, how to bring others to an awareness of it.'*

There is no option once this point has been reached: every artist or medium arriving here enters a new phase. There can be no going back, for chronological time has been relinquished. Even the process of progression is viewed differently.

'The Door marks a turning point in life,' I noted. *'You are moving with the Wheel of Life instead of chronologically. You have to use the energies of learning to grow and expand in different ways to ordinary growth.*

'You must learn to lose the sense of learning in order to become learned. There is no such thing as storing up learning, there is simply different awareness and truth at different points on the circle.

'Everyone whether alive or dead is rooted in a different section of the circle—so all realities are equally real and equally relevant—no one 'reality' is right.'

Since the dawn of history, people have sought to speak with other worlds and gone to adepts who can do it for them. But we might stop here for a moment to examine why. What exactly is it that they want to hear or know? What is the purpose of all this effort? Why do mediumistic Circles gather regularly to facilitate communication? Why even, do spirits which have passed on want to send messages back to the living? Why communicate at all?

This is very much a human need. I explained in another of my books—*Understanding Spirit Guides*—that a very great deal of the communications received by mediums are nothing more than every-day chit-chat, the sort of gossiping irrelevancies that might be exchanged 'over the garden fence'. Needing comfort to help them deal with their grief, the bereaved long to hear once again the familiar voice of their parent or other loved one pronouncing a phrase they recognize, proving, to them at least, that death was not the end and that person still exists in some form, still caring for them in the way they did when alive.

Spiritualist mediums are dedicated to providing this kind of 'evidence' and messages likely to be received in church demonstrations often include references to family celebrations, birthdays, anniversaries, the sharing of memories or information that indicates the communicating spirit is indeed the departed loved one. Proof of survival may involve details the medium (or anyone else) could not possibly know or be aware of; facts or conversations that were never made public;

private and intimate discussions between two people—'evidence of survival' largely consists of information like this.

Though some 'Spirit Guides' may be recognized as elevated beings, most were once human themselves, and as such understand the human need for comfort and reassurance. Communication with the departed also expresses a need for control, for feeling that one can somehow defy the terrors of mortality, breach the boundaries between life and death.

Psychologically too this is valid, for the most terrible thing for an individual to face can sometimes be his own individuality. People are often willing to suffer a great deal to 'belong', to avoid confronting the prospect of their own 'aloneness'.

So far as elevated spirit-forms are concerned, they do not need such methods of communication; they can pass thought straight into another mind—and what is more, elevated spirits do not use the kind of dialogue with which we communicate on Earth. Their thoughts (unlike ours) are examples of complete truth, which is so pure there is no need for comment, argument or discussion. These are likely to be what are referred to as **'teaching guides'**—they do not necessarily facilitate communication with departed relatives or friends but impart works of an inspirational or revelatory nature. In my own case it became obvious over the years that

172

I was granted the means to work on all these levels.

Every individual participating in the act of mediumship has his, her (or even its') own agenda. Groups too may embody specific agendas when they sit in Circles, using the shared energy of all the members to support the medium and achieve communication. There are 'Spirit Rescue' Circles, dedicated to contacting lost or trapped souls. Some Circles work with one particular teaching guide, who passes on philosophical and instructive texts the group can publish or share with others.

This also seems to be the case on the other side. I have found the spirit world seems very anxious that contact should continue to be made and there is generally some response to any request for communication. The agenda here is usually a simple one—to 'prove' the existence of life (sometimes also love) beyond death to the reassurance of those left behind.

The question of agendas—hidden or overtly accepted—is rarely considered by the 'ordinary' person, which is surprising since we live in an age of global advertising and commercial indoctrination on a huge scale. Most religions have their own agenda for the communications they impart. They want their followers to believe what they teach, and this is why personal exploration of dogma or connection with the Divine is discouraged. Even in a physical sense, members of communities too are told how to behave, even how to think, if they want to remain within that community.

Anyone who has ever preferred to think for himself and do his own spiritual journeying to connect with Divine truths has—as we have seen—been regarded as a potentially dangerous subversive and treated with suspicion. Artists, geniuses and visionaries, including mediums, all fall into this category, to whatever extent; they are driven by their burning consciousness of *not* belonging. They are aware of being alone, and their intense need to communicate expresses a desire for higher understanding, for pure truth, a struggling toward the Divine silence in which no words are necessary.

The High Priestess

The High Priestess card in the tarot pack brims with hidden power, secret and intuitive knowledge. The whole point about the Mysteries is that they are just that— mysterious, concealed, only half revealed. Knowledge of the Mysteries—if expressed at all—comes in language unfamiliar and often impossible to understand. This has always been the case. Even when the pronunciations of the priestesses of Delphi were 'translated' they appear to have been double-edged and often meant something quite different from what they seemed to say. This cryptic awareness was necessary in the past—and still is—to keep advanced learning out of the reach of those who would not use it wisely: adherents of the Mysteries were often persecuted.

This kind of empowerment and authority carries huge responsibility. In order to undertake the work you must apply your own discipline, training and preparing yourself to follow a certain way of life. If necessary you voluntarily give up the human condition and its desires and needs—sexual and material gratification, striving in physical time. You aim to achieve the overall picture, to become psychologically detached. To some extent you relinquish the norm, what is regarded as sanity. You edge towards the schizoid, even the autistic. Nothing matters. You have reached the threshold; you are in outer space. Doubts assail you, inexpressible fears undermine you. You cannot relate to what you are told is 'reality'.

Choices have to be made, sacrifices offered. You increasingly cut yourself off from what is regarded as real. You don't know whether you are madder or saner than everyone else. You may refer to psychological theories in order to help those who consult you, but regarding yourself and your own progress you do not start from any known or recognized 'norm'. Your bedrock is the truth as you perceive it: the light of spiritual truth is your only guide.

The isolation and loneliness of working as a medium for Spirit has a positive aspect in that you learn to trust your own insight and intuition; you become extremely self-sufficient mentally and emotionally, the reaction of others, good or bad—including praise directed at you personally—is increasingly irrelevant. But this goes much further: working with Spirit can bring the initiate to a point where, in the words of Elisabeth Haich, he: *'withdraws from the 'fata morgana' of this world and becomes a recluse. However this does not indicate by any means that at this level of consciousness he actually withdraws to a lonely cave. (The symbolism is of) his inner state…he suddenly feels the urge to leave everything and go away…'*

The temptation to devote oneself physically to the spiritual quest can be overwhelming for the medium/priestess. Awareness of the world of Spirit makes the concerns of the 'real' world seem trivial and meaningless. I personally began to find it difficult to relate to the concerns of some who consulted me; my psychic vision focused on their soul journey rather than whether they would get what they wanted or 'be happy' in a material sense.

It was for others struggling along the spiritual path that I felt I was needed, to pass on reassurance from Spirit that was valuable and fulfilling for them in awareness of human mortality and the insignificance of man. But as the years went by I began to be increasingly swept by a painful sadness and distaste for the illusions and shallowness of the world and its concerns. Eventually all my research, study and years of work in the public domain brought me to a point where I felt completely unable to move forward. I noted at the time: *'Strange feeling—no progress—everything has stopped. I have to find out where I am—this is the turning point—the threshold of something else—'.*

I had just completed my latest 'psychic' book—*Understanding Star Children*—where I seemed to have taken my meditations on the nature of psychic striving as far as I could, and would have been repeating myself if I tried to write more. Having explored in some depth that sense of 'otherness', that lack of identification with a progressively more distressing world that makes many individuals feel they do not have, or even want, any part in it, the answer seemed to be that there are no answers.

I could no longer see any way ahead so long as I remained physically 'in' this world. *'But'*, I noted, *'you cannot just give up on living, stop the world and get off.'* So which path should I—or even could I—take when there seemed no way to go?

At the beginning of my psychic career I had been shown a vision of a terrible place of suffering and told that my task was to help the souls struggling there: in order to undertake the task, as I have described elsewhere, I was given the 'burning fire' of spiritual power. I accepted this as my work for Spirit and as a result, spent years working with the public, carrying out thousands of consultations and readings, exploring my own development and writing books about my work.

Then came the turning point, the threshold where I could go no further in a conventional sense. I was ready to move into a quite different phase, a new method of working. Spirit gave me a similar message to the one the medium Rosemary Brown received, as she has recounted in her autobiography *Unfinished Symphonies*. She was told she would be working with a group of musicians in spirit, hopefully for the benefit of humanity. I was told I would—if I accepted the task—also be required to work with several individuals in spirit; I would use my powers as a medium to communicate with them and my skills as a writer, editor and publisher to produce and make available to the public the books that would emerge from our collaboration.

Further than that, I had no idea what was expected of me. The details were unclear, though I felt intuitively that this undertaking would involve the production of at least three books—two would be with my collaborators in spirit and the third, about myself and my mediumship, would provide a kind of 'summing up' of the whole project. Most significantly, however, I foresaw that this would be an undertaking of great difficulty and magnitude that would take years to complete (in fact, it has taken seven).

With such sketchy details it was like being led forward with a blindfold around my eyes, but when Spirit asked whether I would accept this as my path I did not hesitate. The choice was, as it always is, mine to make. I could have refused: but almost without my conscious awareness there was a pivotal, crucial moment when my prayer for guidance was made, the response from Spirit was given and I committed myself to the task. Then I waited for a sign, which came later that day.

Summer with Bax

'In my mind I saw the splashing of great drops of rain,' I noted *'raindrops falling on a wide sheet of water, a lake or the sea, heavy rain, a torrential downpour, cleansing and clearing, powerful and stimulating. This was the image that gave me the first link with Bax...'*

It was the day before the Midsummer Solstice, 2005. I was about to join forces with my first collaborator, the English Romantic composer Sir Arnold Bax, who had died in 1953. I described what happened next in my book *Summer with Bax:*

'Out of the blue, a completely fresh slant on reality presented itself. I met up with another artist—a man who had been a musician, a composer. As a medium I did not seek the gift of communication with other dimensions, but have learned to accept and live with it: when communication was made with Sir Arnold Bax, a celebrated musical giant of the early 20th century, the fact that he had died fifty years previously proved irrelevant. The conversations following our initial contact were vibrantly alive; they revealed new horizons and provided insight into dimensions of experience in ways not normally possible. Reality took a huge, sideways, seismic shift.

'I had been looking for answers in the portentous kind of way that recalled my mother's maxim: 'Life is real, life is earnest'. All that was left behind. Paul (my husband) and I found ourselves experiencing instead an invitation to just stop off and smell the flowers— for appreciation and celebration too, are vital components of living. One can get too involved, become too clever. What a relief it was to start living joyously for a change, forget about trying to solve the problems of humanity—simply to

live in the moment, sharing companionship and laughter, collaborating as a group of friends.'

Paul and I worked throughout the summer with Bax on the material for the new book. It took me into entirely new areas of experience: Spirit raised my mediumship to a level where I found myself able to communicate in direct and sustained trance, recording sittings of up to forty-five minutes at a time, something I had never achieved before.

As the work progressed, all my experience of communicating as a medium became much clearer. No longer does the enquirer need to 'knock on the Door' in order to communicate with the departed in forbidden realms beyond; he is able to recognize that the departed are separated from us only by a shift in perception (possibly, if we were to take this further, unborn spirits who have not yet entered the world can be contacted as well). If the concept is of the Wheel of Life with life/death/between life states/rebirth as just different points on the wheel then death simply marks a change of focus, an altered perspective: one stands in a different place and views the centre point, the 'space between', the 'Moonlit Door' from another angle.

In many magical traditions or philosophies the concept of a symbolic turning point occurs. There is a reversal, whether this is perceived as

181

a death and rebirth or as adopting a viewpoint that 'views from the other side, from the end instead of the beginning'. The new work I was chosen by Spirit to undertake has been based on the awareness of the threshold summarized here:

- At the still point one sees a new world— or a new view of the old world.
- The threshold or Moonlit Door simply marks a shift between the perception of life and the perception of death. *There is no difference between them.*
- It is the place where in ancient tradition there is no time, no beginning, no end, only the moment of awareness.
- At the Door, as in the ancient shrine served by the medium/priestess, access can be gained from any side to the Divine wisdom and truth beyond.
- Everyone needs to move forward but will achieve this in different ways. Some may look as though they are standing still— that is their movement. Communicating with different points on the wheel— different states of being—must also be done in different ways.

'You simply are, and what you are and what you see or feel or connect with
is what the moment holds, which is what music is about. I am neither old nor young, I am

182

neither dead nor alive, I am what I am in the moment.
This is a fascinating thing.'
Romantic composer Sir Arnold Bax
(Through the mediumship of Dilys
Gater in Summer with Bax)

183

The Wheel Turns

In his ground-breaking book *Life After Life*, Dr Raymond A Moody gives many instances of how difficult it is to integrate intense experiences of a spiritual nature into everyday existence. Though he is referring to the emotional impact of the 'Near Death Experience' with its awareness of a wider, better existence, its freedom of vision and intensified sense of truth there is almost always some scenario of this kind in the case of the dedicated initiate or artist: a knowledge, however intuitive, of what it is like on some wonderful 'other side', personal experience of the 'other place' to which the individual longs to return. In cases like these it may be difficult to differentiate between the subject's intense mental activity and what happens to him in physical time and space: the barriers between are likely to be rather blurred.

Like the image of the Wheel of Life, the phases of the moon, the passage of the seasons, we find that we pass through many cycles of learning and development in our lives. Some theories hold that the magical numbers of 7 and 11 govern our progress here on earth, that we progress in 7 and 11 year cycles (which, whether one believes this or not, often turns out to be true).

Equally, there are concepts which present the paradox that the more learned one becomes, the less one knows—and this applies very much in psychic and spiritual work. Other paradoxes are familiar to us in religious teaching: Only by giving away all you have can you become rich.

Mist, can you give me something to hold onto?

Spokes of the wheel. The navigator turns— spinning but also charting a course. Chance is the navigation of O (a symbol for the Divine).

The Pupil
Conversations with Mist

10
THE NOVICE MEDIUM

Interview with Dilys Gater
3 A Personal View

'What is important for the mystic is not belief in the right doctrine but attainment of the true experience. The scientist and the mystic both make experiments in which what has been written is always subordinate to the observation of what is.'

Alan Watts

There is a knocking at the door in the night.
It is someone come to do us harm.
No, it is the three strange angels.
Admit them, admit them

D H Lawrence
Look, we have come through

The Celtic Druids were leaders of their people in magic, spiritual learning, shamanism and healing, the Druid hierarchy also the repository of the wisdom, art and history of the Celts—even the science of its time. There was no written wisdom, the teachings of the Druids being handed down orally, so they were themselves the living embodiments of enlightenment in ancient Celtic times. We no

186

longer have this sense of daily living alongside the wise and enlightened: in a fragmented society there may be no stable, central figures or appreciation of the wisdom of age. The young bow instead to 'peer pressure'.

Unlimited sources of reference are available to all, but though we are bombarded with more immediate, detailed information than has ever before been presented to the human race, much of it is flawed, irrelevant, misleading or deliberately untrue. We are losing any accepted benchmarks against which to measure the validity of the messages we receive, even the sense of reality that should mark what is essentially valuable and meaningful. It is difficult to differentiate between 'true' and 'virtual' in modern society, as well as 'true' and 'correct'.

In former days individuals were too busy coping with full-time survival to worry about what to do with 'quality time', such a thing being unknown to them; too genuinely conscious of the fearful, awesome realities of birth, death and the natural cycles of living to indulge in 'week-end' spirituality. They existed in an uncertain present, seeking advice from their divinities, 'Ancestors' and 'Wise Ones' in prayers that were sincere and genuine, for such guidance was realistically necessary to see them safely through the immediacy of each day. Integrated into their familiar routines, the deities and presences of the Celtic world, like the *lares & penates* of Roman house and hearth, were as much a part of life as the 'Sacred Heart' is now in a Catholic home.

It is with this awareness of a spiritual dimension that exists alongside the physical and is as real and as valid that a medium learns to live day by day. But there are other aspects of this work that are often misunderstood by the general public.

Shouldn't mediumship be something serious and solemn?

I once suggested in the outline of a proposed book about my work that one of the chapters should focus on the irreverence, wit and humour—including one-liners and repartee—I encounter in my dealings with the spirit world. The publisher replied repressively that he did not think there was any place for that sort of thing in such a book. But a lively appreciation of humour is not something discarded when one passes to other realms: any medium can tell you that when communicating with the departed they often find the experience of dying seems to have sharpened many individuals' sense of irony and the ridiculous, particularly if these individuals had not believed in an afterlife.

The novice unprepared for the encompassing completeness of spiritual

188

actuality does not expect spirits or guides of any sort—however dear they might have been in life—to turn up in their familiar sensual, worldly guise. The fact that some 'Guides' are likely to communicate in just the way they would have when they were alive, even down to the odd swear word or two, comes as a refreshing surprise. But souls who have passed into spirit do not basically change. They have the same characteristic quirks of expression and speech, ways of looking at things that marked them as individuals when they were on Earth. They possess the same concerns and cares for those they love, the same awkward and stubborn traits that made them difficult. They are not transformed on death into saints expounding on universal peace and love.

Some spirits I have encountered were so endearingly real it was impossible to mistake them for 'dead'. One gentleman who had passed over ended his communication with his son by saying that though he was aware that spirits often bring images of flowers in a symbolic gesture to their loved ones, he thought that a bit pointless in his son's case. Instead his image was of a bunch of carrots from his allotment, so fresh I could see him shaking the soil from them. 'Far more useful,' he declared.

What kind of guidance should I expect? How do I know it will be right for me?

I was to receive both practical help and instructive guidance of an extremely elevated and widely encompassing nature as I progressed, mainly from Mist but also from other entities which appeared from time to time. All emerged in the easiest possible way, as though they were friends met up with after long absence. Communication usually consisted of informal—even casual—chats: only later could I could appreciate the depth of wisdom imparted. Sometimes I found myself laughing aloud in appreciation of my communicants' wit, being enlightened in the most stimulating companionship I had ever encountered.

My guiding entities and presences have always seemed utterly real in the same way that people I know in a physical sense who are not there in the flesh, are real. They are like tried and tested friends of long standing, members of a close-knit team, companions travelling in the same direction who have come to know, love and understand each other well.

I came to realize that each person's experience of 'Spirit Guides' has to be different. Some mediums may indeed perceive their mentors as awe-inspiring if this is what works best for them, but every individual is guided first and foremost by Spirit to a complete and loving appreciation and acceptance of himself as he really is. In my own case, the joy of coming to know (or be re-united with) close, dearly loved companions with whom I could be as irreverent as I liked as well as appreciating their mental superiority, had blinded me to the truth—that I had been blessed with 'Spirit Guides' prepared to teach and instruct me at every level, not in any rigidly accepted 'right' way but in all the ways that were right for me.

Can you tell me more about your guides— apart from Mist?

During my months in London trying to come to terms with my psychic potential and actively live a spiritual life, I was struggling physically. My health was poor; I was on heavy medication, in constant pain and the prospect of my trials continuing indefinitely was a dismal one for often, it is not the big issues but the niggling discomforts that provide the 'last straw' that really breaks us. Ready to plunge determinedly into confrontation with demons, I could be reduced to tears climbing back-wrenchingly in and out of a car; fighting the panic attacks and palpitations that crippled attempts to assert myself; avoiding my overweight, ageing image in a mirror. I had long found physical existence so difficult

I wanted to be just 'a brain on legs', by the time I began to receive messages from the spirit world during my healing sessions at the Spiritualist Church.

I have already mentioned that I was initially given simple messages to pass on to the healers from sources they identified as departed relatives or friends: in the traditional manner, several were accompanied by images of flowers. But I was not aware of any 'Spirit Guide' participating and seemed to be able to make contact easily and safely without one. Then one day I was given the first clear message for myself from someone in Spirit whom I recognised—though I found difficulty both in accepting his presence in any sort of mystical connection and in casting him (of all people) in the role of spiritual adviser.

Throughout my twenties I had had a close relationship with a much older man who had been my colleague, mentor, lover and friend. A vibrantly alive personality, he was not particularly spiritual—had not believed in an afterlife so far as I recall—but to my amazement it was he who was coming through during my healing sessions at the Church. He took me back to a specific place and time that had meant a lot to me: the city of Chester in the Spring of the first year we had known each other. The pink and white of flowering blossom trees had marked the beginning not only of the kind of passionate liaison most

192

people only dream about, but also my career as a writer, which he had helped to foster and encourage. The same presence and visions returned for some weeks, every time I went back to the Church for healing, until I could accept and understand the message—not passed on in words as such but in the ways that would become familiar to me, as images and thought patterns entering my mind.

Everything had been before me that Spring when we met. I had been young and (even if I say it myself) lovely, talented and confident in my ability to challenge fate and conquer the world. Now, tired and ill, I had just suffered the break-up of a third marriage leaving me alone with no resources and perhaps worst of all, the writing career on which my living depended was going through a bad patch.

The spirit world revealed itself to me in those early communications as first and foremost immensely practical, giving evidence of how lovingly Spirit cares for all our needs. I was not removed from the Earth plane, levitated onto a heavenly cloud with a saintly being to instruct me. Instead I received solid reassurance from a 'man of the world' I had trusted and loved to help me in the most material of ways. Cosmic warfare and battles with the dark did not cripple me as much as my human fears and most pressing physical problems—pain, lack of confidence, even the chronic state of my finances and business dealings. This particular person had 'been there' in these respects for me during those earlier Spring days in Chester: he was exactly the person to lift me now when I was lost and vulnerable.

But it was difficult to regard him as anything so portentous and formal as a 'Spirit Guide'— and I am sure he would have considered such a title the most tremendous joke. His still-living presence with me seemed altogether so far-fetched and unlikely that it took years before I felt I could reveal to anyone how he had come through from 'beyond the Veil' with the practical help I needed so badly. His message—as his words had always been in life—was grounding and reassuring. He told me to open my eyes, look beyond my personal preoccupations and stop clinging to my fear and distress. Once again it was the Spring of the year, and the blossom trees in London were coming out—one was in full glorious bloom outside the Church.

'Yes, our time—that time we shared—was wonderful but it has gone so let it go. This Spring is just as real and this is your own, for you. Take it and enjoy it, live in this moment. Though things are very different now, not what you expected, this is your time for a new blossoming, a new beginning.'

Since my first days as a medium this particular 'guide' has stayed with me and been there whenever I have needed his humour and companionship, his practical advice and assistance. When I asked him how it was possible that he, who did not even take the spiritual seriously, had come to 'be there' for me, this was the answer I received, with no further explanation:

'You needed an angel, didn't you? Why shouldn't there be an angel in a grey business suit?'

Cassandra's message of hope

One memorable entity made itself known to me only once, very early on when I was still in the process of making contact with possible 'Spirit Guides' and before I encountered Mist. I have never known whether this particular being was a man or a woman. I sensed the presence of a male personality rather than a female but when I asked for a name I was given 'Cassandra'—the prophetess who in Greek myth foretold the fall of Troy.

The story goes that the god Apollo fell in love with Cassandra and promised her the gift of prophecy if she would yield to his advances. She said yes and the gift was granted but she then perversely changed her mind and refused him. The frustrated Apollo warned her that though she would indeed be able to prophesy truthfully, as a punishment for going back on her word her prophecies would never

195

be believed.

This is not an altogether uncommon fate for those who 'see' and try to share their visions and I wonder if perhaps my uncertainty over 'Cassandra's' identity underlines the point that regardless of their sex, anyone speaking the unwelcome truth about what is to come can find themselves regarded as a 'doom and gloom' merchant.

'Cassandra' certainly seemed to be preoccupied with doom—with a capital D! He or she only held one long 'conversation' with me and in spite of my efforts I was never able to contact him/ her again. But the conversation was extremely interesting since it had something to say about a subject most responsible people find it difficult to make sense of—the distressing evils that appear to prevail within our world.

'Cassandra's' words reflect the sort of outrage and disgust we all feel sometimes but they remind us that all things work their way through, everything passes its destined course. The tragedies we think are more than we can stand, the blows that seem to mark the end of our world have happened before and will happen again—this is the concept of cyclic progression most spiritual teachings present. Even the most wonderful moments cannot last. There has to be a constant forward movement to hold the balance between the polarities, between positive and negative, good and evil.

From the 'Cassandra' text

I found myself in a time and a place where there was idolatry of the loud and the crass and the nihilistic and the minds of the multitudes like lemmings rushed without awareness to their destruction. The end of the world has come as it came then to me and to those around me. O if only the very stones of Ninevah and Crassia and Poseidon could speak, they would cry out and say that in the midst of the sound there is only the hollow rattle of approaching death, and the skull shakes as a gourd and rattles. For there comes a time when the spirit has flickered so low that the flame is almost extinguished, and it is then that the multitude rattles together and the sound is like a torment that beats the light into madness and death.

What shall be done, and what could they do?

O without delay, seek the stony place and the bleak and bare path that is empty and where there is no sound, and hold the moment and the stillness. O weep not, nor cry where shall we go, for the stony place is within, and the path beneath the feet of every spirit.

O let the viands of filthiness and pigs swilling their troughs go, and see that even the pigs are creatures of inner clean, and see rather the lowest of predators snorting in their rotting remains and in the excrement and vomit, and,

197

unaware, saying: This is richness. Lift the stained snout from such outrage in the face of the flames of divinity, and kneel for the drops of living water.

O like the water to a soul that is at the moment of extinction is the peace of the stony place, and to me. Many times I came to this moment, to the lifting of my head to see the multitudes illuminated in the sulphurous flames of a living hell, their blues and reds, and I saw them and stood among them and said: How came I here, and wherefore?

I am sick with the old, old sickness that again I must stand to watch the death throes of the god flames, and I ask why, o why must this be so? It is so far from the pearls of living water, the coolness and smoothness, the essence of purity and stillness.

Spiritual teachings sometimes need to be uncomfortably couched in language that will hit home. If we will not confront the truth— however upsetting—and face the real reasons why we need reassurance and comfort, we can never be realistically comforted.

We know that life seems to provoke the same questions 'Cassandra' asks so passionately: why does ugliness and horror exist, why are terrible things allowed to happen, why must living break our hearts? Some things are so hurtful that they seem to rub out all sense of the beautiful and the good. How is it possible to live, to want to live when we must accept the extremes of evil, depravity and cruelty that exist?

Alongside the questions the answer is also given. It is up to each individual soul to make its own decision about the reality in which it will choose to live, what it will value and recognize and uphold. But 'Cassandra' perhaps speaks for all of us in asking 'How?' and 'Why?' and 'What for?'

There was more in this interview that I found extremely thought-provoking:

I am the watcher at the gate of hell. I am the one granted the vision too late to be believed. I was called at one time, Cassandra. I wept and tore my hair, and gave my own flame to help the others, but they have no ears and I learned it was useless. I do not come until the rattle is in the throat and death is imminent. I am the Mourner for I feel for the pity and the waste, and I am the Light Bearer to be there when the rattles cease and the small god flames turn in fearful bewilderment and look for assistance.

I asked: Is this hell then, here and now?

What else? Hell is not a place to which the soul goes, it is a place which comes and seeks admittance and is received joyously and makes its home within the head and the heart. And hell is not cruelty and pain, it is the slow eroding away of all that makes up the god light; it is blankness and the eroding of all true sensation of the mind so that there is no difference between the things of seeming richness and the offal.

For there walk among the sheep many beasts with ravening jaws slobbering blood, and no man sees or knows, and the laughter is the same for each death as for the coloured balls spinning in the air.

Cassandra's' highly motive pronunciations can seem frightening (as well as incomprehensible) to minds unused to prophetic utterance and fire-and-brimstone oratory. I usually refer sitters who are lost in dread and despair to the easier to understand parallels we can draw from the tarot card called the Ten of Swords. This represents the heaviest of all burdens that have to be carried in life, the sort of things that can seem like a real 'end of our world' where everything is lost and nothing can get any worse. But when you are as low as you can be and have faced the worst possible scenario there is, the future can actually appear quite cheerful by comparison. There is only one way left to go and that is—up!

Are you afraid of dying?

All human beings are. It is programmed into us. At the same time as giving us life—our bodies are indeed mostly composed from water—we have seen that we visualize the boundaries between life and death as marked by dark, mysterious rivers we will have to cross to reach the Underworld, abode of the dead. This shadowy kingdom is dangerous territory, forbidden for mortals to tread, but it is the medium's and the artist's privilege to venture into this gloomy landscape—or at least to glimpse it.

Artistic expression of this concept is everywhere, sometimes obliquely or through images, sometimes directly. Death is one of the favourite themes of poets, a kind of enjoyable morbidity we start to relish in adolescence. Most articulate and artistic teenagers will at some time or another compose works of art— poems or paintings—about death and dying and of course it is wonderfully expressed by the greats. D H Lawrence wrote in his poem *The Ship of Death*:

Have you built your ship of death, O have you?
O build your ship of death, for you will need it.

Already the dark and endless ocean of the end
is washing in through the breaches of our

201

wounds, already the flood is upon us.
Oh build your ship of death, your little ark
and furnish it with food, with little cakes,
and wine
for the dark flight down oblivion.

How many death scenes are there in opera, in literature? The subject is something we consciously explore in our most intense and passionate moments of living. I wrote in *The Urban Shaman:*

'Entry into Otherworlds, particularly the Underworld, is through physical cracks, holes in the ground to animal paths that disappear in darkness, strange and mysterious gateways, hidden doorways, places where the veil is thin. The journey is often represented symbolically as part of a hunting process—the hunt atavistically identified with sexual activity, mating, procreation of the species as well as visionary enlightenment. In the ballet stories of Giselle *and* Swan Lake, *hunting is the means by which the seekers achieve, through painful suffering, the ultimate fulfillment of desire and love. In hunter-related cultures such as that of the ancient Celts, an animal may appear to lead or guide the hunter—traditional figures of this kind are mythological beasts such as a unicorn or white stag.'*

The truth is that humanity is fascinated by

202

the prospect of its own death, especially if emotively or artistically presented; but at the same time it assures itself robustly that 'it will never happen to me'. This double-edged fascination extends to the activities of people perceived as inhabiting the twilight landscape between life and death—mediums or artists. They, it is felt, are familiar with the creepy horrors of crypts and graves and can pass on information that saves the 'ordinary' person having to venture into such places himself. But at the same time, there is the comforting reassurance that one does not have to take what they say seriously.

Have you, as a medium, any personal thoughts on death?

Well, the image of death is a terrifyingly familiar one in western spiritual teaching. The Grim Reaper—a skeleton wielding a scythe; or an armed warrior on a white horse. Jonathan Dee points out in his book on Tarot that: *'The symbol of Death as an armed warrior is taken from the Book of Revelation: Behold a pale horse and his name that sat on him was death, and hell followed after him'.*

It is a very scary prospect, death. Whether good or bad, it marks the final awful point where whatever beliefs it might have had in life, the human soul loses all control and has to abandon itself to whatever does actually lie beyond, existence in some form other than the physical body. For those who have been brought up within some form of Christianity, there is also likely to be a sense of guilt and sin inducing fear that what waits is hell—eternal suffering and punishment, however this is perceived—horrifying enough, but even worse when the soul is stripped of its very self, the identity with which it has been familiar throughout its whole conscious journey through life.

No wonder that in its naked vulnerability, the soul clings to the concept of heaven, paradise, all ways of visualizing final metamorphosis and union with the Divine which offer a more hopeful outcome: the stillness and peace that has been so desperately and intuitively sought while struggling through the physical world. This idea is so subjective and personal there is no one way to describe it, especially since there is no possible means of gaining enlightenment except by actually dying oneself.

In my experience as a medium, the idea of actual union with the Divine, the Source, is something that lies so far beyond our physical death that we must discount it. In our ignorance and arrogance we may aspire to this kind of union, but it would be more realistic to hope instead—at this point in life's journey—for union with our spiritual guides, angelic beings or what is referred to as our Higher Selves when we go 'beyond the Veil'. The paintings of William Blake, mysterious and disturbing, show life essence as beings of light, and illustrate shining forms flowing and merging. This is perhaps the sort of union awaiting us.

I have already mentioned that I first 'saw' my guide Mist as 'a silver man with no face' seemingly encased in silver armour of some kind, including a visor obscuring the head and features. Apparently the image of an armed warrior-knight has also marked the early communications of other mediums: Rosemary Brown, for instance, describes in *Unfinished Symphonies* her first visitation of an astral being at the age of six or seven:

'I saw what appeared to be a knight in beautiful shining armour standing over me with a sword held upright above his head. He was so beautiful and there was such an air of peace and calm about him…I felt certain he was some kind of guardian angel standing over me…'

She also adds that: *'Years later I read in the* Psychic News *that a very famous medium Estelle Roberts…had a very similar experience,'* and there may well have been others I am not aware of, as the archetypal image of a knight in shining armour is one of the most potent in the western world.

When I first 'saw' Mist I was aware of great power but made no connection with the horsemen of the Apocalypse, more with the knights of Arthurian romance. However, as I progressed in awareness it became more and more apparent that any forms of spiritual power, whether for 'good' or 'evil', would of course present themselves to the human senses in some suitable, appropriate shape or guise.

Since the Apocalypse is seen from a human point of view as the disaster beyond all disasters, what more appropriate than a vision of mounted and armed warriors, which at most periods of history would have been the most terrifying image possible as marking The End—whether the end of the world or the end of our individual selves. These are not the same thing, though in metaphysical speculation we cannot actually be sure whether the world would continue to go on without us. We see how it goes on after other people have passed over, but if we are not here in person to know about it, can we be certain life on Earth would really continue, the sun would rise and set and the years follow each other beyond the date of our death?

As a child needs to be taught the many different aspects of living in a material world, so the medium/priestess needs to learn that there is far more to life after death than the simplistic 'black-and-white' images of popular belief. We do not just die and go to heaven or hell and that is that. Neither do we 'go out' like a candle flame. There may be many heavens or hells, many further stages of our soul's journey. So the terrifying/reassuring visions of armed warriors who assist in bringing about necessary change or transformation, whether perceived by the soul as good or bad, can be viewed as welcome guides or barbaric enemies, depending on our state of spiritual maturity.

'... death is necessary in order to make a fresh start. We must allow the old to pass away so that we can usher in the new. Initiation into the mysteries involves the death of one's old self... This cycle of death and rebirth is the essential theme of the alchemical process.'

Rosemary Ellen Guiley and Robert M Place
The Alchemical Tarot

Can we achieve any sort of union or transcendence while here on Earth?

'... the card of Death can also symbolize change, but of a transforming kind, the passage through ordeal to some sort of rebirth. All the mystery cults of antiquity initiated their members by some kind of ceremony in which they enacted death and rebirth'

Brian Innes
The Tarot: How to Use and Interpret the Cards

When Dion Fortune wrote *The Training & Work of an Initiate* in 1930 describing the aims and ideals of her famous school, the Fraternity of the Inner Light, she mentions at one point the duties of her initiates 'as knights of God'—again that archetypal image of an armed warrior. She also describes her concept of the Initiate as: '*...one in whom the Higher Self, the Individuality, has coalesced with the personality and actually entered into incarnation with the physical body. An Initiate, therefore, is one whose Higher Self it is that looks out at us through his eyes. The personality is reduced to a set of habit-complexes of living, leaving the Higher Self free to carry on its work with the minimum demands upon its attention from the physical plane.*'

Whether one describes the Initiate's years of training as in occultism, neopaganism, Christian mysticism or—as I have done in this book—the dedication and training of the medium/priestess or even the artist—the process is still one of integration, through various stages, with the Higher Self, however this presents itself. Though I personally am not physically dead, the work I have done over the years with Mist has revealed how as I became more aware, I achieved a certain amount of integration with 'his' power and strength, which cannot be fully accomplished while I remain in a physical body.

I wrote this poem after experiencing a vision of the agony of 'flowing' into a much loved spirituality and being dragged back by my own physicality. (This also expresses the yearning of the artist to capture or recreate the unity of his artistic and transcendental visions). I titled it *Astral Sex* but it really illustrates how sexuality ceases to exist when the soul leaves the body behind.

Racing the ocean's surface,
Two great waves thunder,
Mingle, enmesh, swell,
Eternal.

No separateness, no together.
No rejection, no belonging.
No I, no you, no us.
Just.

But my first cry, from the human heart,
All human senses transcended,
The childish frustration bitter in my mouth,
'Oh, even as the great waves thunder,
Each within the other, each the other,
The other each, time without end,
Yet I have no hands now, no arms, no lips.
Oh, you are here, you have come
But I cannot kiss you, I cannot hold you.
I cannot touch.'

Racing the ocean's surface,

> *Two great waves thunder,*
> *Mingle, enmesh, swell,*
> *Eternal.*
>
> *No separateness, no together.*
> *No rejection, no belonging.*
> *No I, no you, no us.*
> *Just.*

Some of Emily Bronte's poetry—whatever her original intentions, which are still being debated by scholars—also seems to me to wonderfully describe the ecstatic joy and physical pain of this process:

> *'Listen, 'tis just the hour,*
> *The awful time for thee;*
> *Dost thou not feel upon thy soul*
> *A flood of strange sensations roll,*
> *Forerunners of a sterner power,*
> *Heralds of me? ...*
>
> *Oh dreadful is the check,—intense the*
>   *agony,*
> *When the ear begins to hear and the eye*
>   *begins to see;*
> *When the pulse begins to throb, the brain*
>   *to think again,*
> *The soul to feel the flesh and the flesh to feel*
>   *the chain...'*

Often mediums describe how as they

progress they feel they 'become' their guides (or Higher Selves.). I experienced this as a very distinct and upsetting sense of intense loss. I was carrying out my training as a Reiki Master at the time, and told my own Master in some distress: 'I kept feeling Mist coming nearer and nearer. It was amazing and wonderful. He came so very close. And now I don't know what has happened—I can't seem to find him.'

'Perhaps,' suggested my Master gently. 'He has gone within.'

But I did not want to think Mist had 'gone within'. I wanted the relationship to stay as it had always been—that I could turn to someone stronger and wiser to give me all the answers instead of having to 'look within' and find them myself. It was only when I was able to accept that sense of personal responsibility that I 'found' Mist again but in a new and different relationship based on equality and mutual dependence and trust. I learned that we cannot simply expect our guides to 'be there' and keep giving with no reciprocal offering back. They need whatever we can give to them—in my case, as I have explained, I dedicated myself anew to serving Spirit in whatever task I might be given to undertake. I pledged myself to the service of Spirit as the most important—indeed, the only—thing in my life that mattered.

I was given this incredibly beautiful communication from my guide—and I am sure others who reach a similar stage of development will experience the same reassurance from their own guiding presences, whatever form it may take.

Mist's promise

the End is the Beginning, in the light of true awareness

We are one and nothing can part us, neither the sea or the storm, the rocks or the tempest, the compass needle or the dial of the sunclock; we are the waves of the sea which have met and intermingled and become one great wave: I am you and you are me.

Do not fear, for we travel into the ocean of beyond where the every-days cannot follow. You are mine in the everlasting of eternities, shifting as clouds and constant as the moon, your face to mine, your arms my arms, your breath giving me life.

If there is love, my darling, it is not the pearly drops of human existence, it is the stars, galaxy after galaxy, into infinity, and myself within you. This is yourself, know me, feel me, recognize me as I know you. I have been only a part, drifting until the waves met, now you are within me, the waters filled, my fingers within yours trailing weed, my mouth yours.

212

Know this and know me.

Can you make any comment on what happens to those who commit Suicide?

I have many times been consulted by people whose relatives or close friends died through some form of suicide—drowning, hanging, asphyxiation. They are very sad cases, and the contacts established have always reflected this sense of bewilderment and confusion.

I have never experienced a clear-cut response of 'Yes, I did it because I wanted to die, and now I am dead so that is that'. On some occasions the spirits concerned appear to be unaware themselves of what their motivation was, and may indicate things 'went wrong' or happened 'accidentally'. In other cases the fact that death occurred seems to have clarified problems the individual was suffering in life—for example, one particularly striking example I encountered concerned a young man who had apparently been living a wild lifestyle of 'sex, drugs and rock 'n' roll' before he hanged himself.

His ashes ended up on the mantelpiece of his former partner's flat (he had been gay) where, I was informed, they were sometimes mingled with the ashes from a 'joint'. His spirit made contact in great distress, needing the

213

consolation of traditional funeral rites, the solemn dignity of a 'proper' grave' with floral tributes—all the sense of communal caring that he and his friends had so contemptuously rejected. His existence seemed to have lacked purpose and meaning, the importance of which he realized and requested in death. He felt himself isolated and wanted to be accepted and mourned by the community, able at last to draw on their ancient and atavistic strength.

My experience of spirits which have passed as a result of suicide reinforces this sense of terrible isolation and most usually reflects the legal phrase 'disturbed balance of mind'. The spirits seem trapped in painful experience like a fly in amber. They are generally inarticulate and seem to have been suffering greatly when they took their lives. Some hardly know which world they are in. My impression is that suicide happens under huge pressure that offers the individual no other option—they feel there is literally nothing else they can do and they pass helpless to their doom.

I sense no judgment on them. But they are not allowed to by-pass the responsibilities which confront every soul. In my experience these immature spirits are able to lay down their terrible burdens in the 'neutral zone' and recover their strength—taking as much time as they need—but they will inevitably have to begin again, refocusing their attention once more on completing their essential journey

214

through an earthly life.

Do you have any further comment on how you view your role now?

My given name Dilys (which is Welsh) is like the French *fleur-delys* and signifies 'purity'. In my Welsh dictionary *dilys* is an adjective meaning 'sure, certain, genuine', the noun *dilysrwydd* means 'genuine'; the verb *dilysu* as 'to certify, warrant or guarantee'. My unusual name has always marked me out—something I found disconcerting as a girl—but I have come to regard it as a 'badge of office' defining how I now view both my role and the obligations I am committed to fulfil.

PART FOUR
EXPLORING THE THRESHOLD
'We shall go forward together...We shall open the gates...'

'All art is one, and there is no difference in the mystery of the craft,
only in the hand and eye of the craftsman.'

Michael Powell, film director

'Art is action—and it's moral action...
There is no way that art can separate itself
from what we have to go through in this world
as human beings.'

Alice Goodman
Librettist—*The Death of Klinghoffer*

'... this place is a house of justice but also of
retribution and death...
Realizing that you do not have a fear of the truth
brings a clearing of the air and an alignment
with...superior intelligences.'

T. Mann
Tarot

217

The Travellers

Who are the travellers on this journey to 'the place'—whatever it may prove to be? You realize you are one of them: many people on different roads, travelling alone even though they may appear to be travelling together.

Where are they travelling? As with the word 'Dinas', other words may mean different things to different people. What is the difference, in the end, between the visions of the mystic, the artist or the shaman? All struggle to transcend themselves, to loosen the bonds of physicality and achieve a wider, richer, more elevated existence.

A man's personality need not end on reaching the door of death. It could be but the beginning of a further 'pilgrim's progress' of the soul. The Spiritualist vision of a beautiful 'Summerland' beyond death—or even a more sombre 'Winterland'—is a simplistic image like the Christian Heaven and Hell, but these are images that make it easier for some people to visualize than an abstract concept of simply moving forward—or moving on in whichever way.

And it is the concept of the journey that matters here, the idea too that the traveller will encounter guides along the way. The Native Americans communicated with trees—'the Standing People'—who nurtured them. The Celts and many others revered the inhabitants of the upper and lower worlds—the 'gods', the animals, the ancestors—who provided comfort, inspiration and wise advice. Always the human race has looked to its visionaries and mystics, its artists, its shamans, for signposts to help and guide them.

From my notes

11
TEAM WORK

'Who will come with me to the edge of the world?'
Sir Arnold Bax
(Through the mediumship of Dilys Gater in Summer with Bax)

'The dead don't die. They look on and help.'
D H Lawrence

In the 1970s Rosemary Brown, a London housewife, achieved international fame when she was the recipient of music scores 'dictated' to her by a group of composers who had passed over: the group included Brahms, Chopin, Schubert, Beethoven, Bach, Debussy and Rachmaninov. Her main contact and spokesperson for the group was Franz Liszt, who remained in communication with her for many years and who is quoted extensively in her autobiography *Unfinished Symphonies*. She became known world-wide, her 'astral music' performed on radio, TV and records.

The stated objective of the group of musicians who chose to work with her as their mouthpiece and representative, was to *'establish a precept for humanity, ie. that physical death is a transition from one state of consciousness to another wherein one retains one's individuality.'*

'To understand himself fully,' claimed another spokesperson for the group, musician and composer Sir Donald Tovey, *'he (Man) should become aware of the fact that he does not consist merely of a temporary form which is doomed to age and die. He has an immortal soul which is housed in an immortal body and endowed with a mind that is independent of the physical brain.'*

Similar messages from those in spirit—whether as groups or individuals—have been made available by mediums from the dawn of civilization. Holy texts are full of them. Cases of 'seers' or 'prophets' offering 'inspired' advice and admonition (whether genuine or fraudulent) litter the pages of history.

What was different about Rosemary Brown was that her communicators 'dictated' their works to her as musical notes, which she had to transcribe onto the staves of manuscript paper. Since she did not read music herself, every bar of the intricate working had to be described to her in minute detail.

At about the same period, a young man called Matthew Manning published his book *The Link: The Extraordinary Gifts of a Teenage Psychic*. Included in the book were examples of

221

the artwork granted to Matthew by automatic writing—purporting to be from a large number of diverse artists including Picasso, Albrecht Durer, Aubrey Beardsley, Paul Klee, the Elizabethan miniaturist Isaac Oliver and Leonardo da Vinci.

Matthew Manning—like Rosemary Brown—had been aware of his psychic gifts and powers since an early age, though his initially took the form of disturbing poltergeist activity. Interestingly, he was not described at that time as a medium. The blurb on the cover of a paperback edition of his book published later in 1987, explains it 'made headlines, for its subject was able to produce examples of most types of psychic phenomena known to researchers, including metal bending (which earned him the title 'England's answer to Uri Geller'), major poltergeist phenomena at home and school (which almost got him expelled), automatic writing, remarkable psychic drawings and paintings; accurate medical diagnoses purporting to come from a long-dead doctor who called himself William Penn, and precognition.'

Also like Rosemary Brown, Matthew Manning allowed himself and his psychic abilities to be tested by experts and scientists. In both cases, in spite of the fact that their gifts appeared to be perfectly genuine, with an incredible body of evidence to back them up, the Establishment in general was content

222

to pronounce a verdict of 'not proven', much as I had done about supernatural activity myself before I consciously set out on my own spiritual journey.

Time magazine commented: *'Everyone loves a mystery. Whichever side one takes on the question of communication with the dead, Rosemary is clearly a musical mystery.'*

Dr A R G Owen, Fellow of Trinity College, Cambridge, Geneticist, Biologist and Mathematician, Director of The New Horizons Research Foundation, Toronto, contributed a report on Matthew's psychic abilities, which he had observed and tested, in *The Link*.

'...I am inclined to say there is quite a case for supposing Matthew receives information by paranormal means. Whether this is actually from the spirits of the dead I cannot say... Whichever interpretation one chooses to adopt (ie: in the field of human survival of death or extrasensory perception) ...there remain many mysteries and loose ends... Many psychic persons content themselves with mere repetitions of their paranormal effects and this perhaps is one of the reasons why parapsychology advances only slowly. But if Matthew can continue to combine the exercise of his powers with the same spirit of enquiry that he has already shown, it is likely that his work may lead to a new and profound scientific insight into these matters.'

I said at the beginning of this book that I took it for granted that my readers are already aware *'that there are dimensions beyond our own, and will not want to waste time speculating about existence after death or whether souls survive'*. But I have mentioned these two cases because they have something in common with my own experience. Each medium was dealing with a group—or groups—of departed spirits wanting to communicate. Each was dealing with creative artists—who, unlike more 'ordinary' communicants, might be expected to have some particularly original, interpretive or artistic view of life and death to offer.

When I set to work in 2005 preparing the material for what was to become *Summer with Bax*, I found myself doing the same. Following Spirit's instructions and with assistance from my husband Paul, who provided the factual background chapters about Sir Arnold Bax's life, I began communicating with the composer.

'A 'mental medium', Dilys makes contact with the world of spirit by focusing her concentration; no dimmed lights, sitting in circles or special conditions are required. For the sessions described in this book, she and her co-author/ researcher husband Paul 'simply sat down quietly with a tape recorder', reported the Introduction to the book.

Regarding the actual procedure of

mediumship, she explains: 'I had prepared myself on a deeper level for some days before each session, carrying out internal disciplines that naturally, were not visible to anyone else. When we came to do the sessions, I sat comfortably relaxed, closed my eyes and passed into a light trance. I connected within minutes with Bax, and just spoke aloud the communications he gave me. Because I am not a 'direct voice' medium, my voice does not change, so the results (all of which are preserved in our files) sound as though I am holding a conversation on the phone, relaying messages and comments from the other end.'

'The three of us each did our bit, and the results must be taken on their own merit—but Paul and I want to emphasise that any flaws or weaknesses have occurred at our end, and not where some of the most interesting concepts originated, with Bax. Far from being a grim kind of 'message from the dead', we found his contributions a unique and vital wake-up call to life, a testament to the great joy and wonder of being alive in our beautiful world.

Carrying out and recording the sessions of mediumship, transcribing the material, researching, writing and editing the book took nearly a year and it was published by our publishing imprint Anecdotes in 2006. We gave it a Book Launch as part of the Buxton

225

Music Festival Fringe in July, 2006.

The Bax book was subtitled: *A Fresh Take on Reality.* His five long sessions of communication with us showed us how an artist sees the world—in his case he presented a view of life as music. This was hardly surprising since he was a Late Romantic composer of a wide range of orchestral, choral and chamber music. He was noted for the emotional colour, depth and passion of his work. A virtuoso pianist, he was also a gifted writer, raconteur and wit.

His energy was phenomenal; we could feel it buoying us up as we worked on the manuscript.

'*Who will come with me to the edge of the world?*' was his challenge.

We found ourselves exploring the dimensions of life and death in unexpectedly inspiring and illuminating ways, I wrote. *We were given insight into the many facets of the creative process, whether the creation was of an abstract work of art or music—or just the day to day shaping of the individual's own existence here in the 'real' world.*

This is not the first time Bax has made contact with us—or we with him, for it is sometimes difficult to identify whether communication with the spiritual world is initiated by the medium or by the communicator. With hindsight, and in

226

view of how this book has come into being, we have concluded that Bax might have been trying to communicate his thoughts and messages for some time and been seeking an appropriate mouthpiece...

Our first contact took place some years ago, when Paul was struggling with his writing career. I found myself linking in to Bax in order to ask for his thoughts on artistic endeavour. With no clear idea of what he had looked like, I perceived the composer at this time as an elderly man, sitting at a desk in what seemed to be a library or study—even a music room, since there was a grand piano. Apparently the setting was some large country house. There were long windows with sunny green lawns outside. Often, a communicating spirit will present itself in what it feels to be the most appropriate form—so in view of the dynamic, youthful personality I was later to come to know, it seems likely that on first contact Bax must have felt he needed to put across a suitably dignified, 'elder statesman' kind of impression.

This first encounter was not a success. When Paul (through me) tried to frame questions about composing, writing and artistic work in general, Bax sharply implied Paul was wasting his time. Paul, in his turn, took offence. If it had been possible between two worlds, I think they might have come to blows. Paul did the equivalent of stamping out of the room, though I managed to persuade him to return in another session and apologize. On the whole though, Bax was not impressed and the contact seemed to have come to nothing.

Time and place were not then appropriate. Even though I would have been able to function as a medium for Bax, I needed to develop further so far as my own work and my books were concerned, while Paul was not equipped then to provide the collaboration that was needed.

By the time we met up again and this book (ie: Summer with Bax) *took shape, we had moved to live in a different and far more liberating environment. Paul had written two books exploring spiritual subjects that had radically changed his outlook on life, and I had reached a point where I was spiritually 'written out' and needed to consider some completely original, fresh 'take' on reality. We were ready for change, ready to consider whatever new options might present themselves.*

Bax was to reveal the way forward....

A Season with Vivien Leigh

I had been told I would be working with several individuals in spirit, and all the time I was in communication with Bax I was aware of the shadowy figure of a woman waiting patiently 'in the wings' until her turn came. Almost from the beginning, I knew intuitively that she was an actress—though at first, I thought a dancer—but was not sure of her identity until the first book was finished and I could concentrate on the second.

I felt that the woman seemed to have some connection with Bipolar Disorder (or Manic Depression, as it was known in the past) from which I also suffer. I wondered briefly whether it was Jessie Matthews, the much-loved star of the English stage and screen, who also suffered from Bipolar Disorder. Eventually, however, she revealed herself as the beautiful and gifted English actress Vivien Leigh, who had always fascinated me since I saw her as a girl in *Gone With The Wind*.

She presented herself extremely dramatically—initially as though she was sitting in a theatre Dressing Room, being interviewed by a journalist (that was my role); and later standing alone in the dusk in falling snow, at the gateway to a graveyard similar to the huge London cemeteries like Hampstead or Brompton (which I knew well and often visited when I lived in London.) She was wearing a fur coat, with a bunch of violets or some purple flowers pinned at her breast—I discovered later that she was very susceptible to the cold and always travelled with her mink coat. This image of the graveyard gates proved, as we progressed, to be a 'stage set' rather than any real place.

Following on the publication of *Summer with Bax,* I worked for the next year in communication with this lovely and iconic star on the book that became *A Season with Vivien Leigh.* The methods by which she chose to communicate were different to those of Bax. Paul recorded two long sessions of trance mediumship to begin with, but she indicated at that point that she would prefer to 'dictate' her notes to me alone. I had to remain 'on call' for her at all times; usually she would wake me up in the early hours of the morning and I would scribble her dictation in longhand, typing it up later. The fact that she had been an insomniac may have accounted for this.

I wrote and researched this book alone with no co-author, and it appeared in 2007, again under our Anecdotes imprint. Again we held a Book Launch as part of the Buxton Festival Fringe in July.

The subtitle of the 'Vivien Leigh book' was: *The Life and Art of an Actress,* though I had originally thought of subtitling it: *The Struggle for Sanity.* While Bax had been incredibly uplifting to work with, this collaboration was painful and difficult, as I explained in the Introduction:

This second book was very different both in the approach and the writing—so different that if

I had not broken the ice, as it were, with Bax, I doubt whether I would have dared to attempt it. The communications came through in a much vaguer, more fragmented form; they did not seem to make sense, and I was working in the dark for a great deal of the time.

I tried to keep my own impressions and opinions out—which you have to do as a medium—but I discovered that this communicator actually required input from me. She needed encouragement and support—not just a straightforward 'secretary to dictate to', but someone to help her clarify her thoughts as she went along—prompt her, as it were, keep her focused. And she wanted more than that too: a great deal of physical energy, so much that she exhausted me almost to the point of nervous collapse.

A lot of what she said came in note form. I even wondered at one stage whether the whole thing was meant to be a kind of teaching notebook on acting, the book Vivien Leigh never wrote in her lifetime. It took a long time—for her too, I think—to work out the structure in detail and I spent literally months transcribing everything, moving the sections around to find the way she wanted to present them. I researched and wrote reams of background material, then had to discard most of it leaving just enough—I hope—to support and clarify the text as it was communicated. Editing and collating all the material eventually resulted in a final form very

231

much decided by Miss Leigh herself.

When a book like this appears, I added, *there are several questions likely to be asked apart from obvious queries about how the procedure works. Why did the communicator make contact? And why did he/she make contact with this particular medium?*

In order for communication to be made, the most appropriate medium has to be found. Because of the special circumstances of this woman's life—her illness and all it involved—she had to have someone who could understand what she was talking about. During her lifetime she was very much an outsider, as anyone who suffers severe mental disorder is bound to be: the average man in the street—even the average medium—has little or no experience of what it is like living with this kind of affliction. Because I have suffered from mental illness myself, even though not to the same degree, I was able to follow her mind intelligently, I hope, into the dark and shadowy areas she wanted to explore.

Where Bax revealed that life could be viewed as music, as artistic creation, Vivien showed us that you can turn life upside down to make sense of it. Her book explored the realities of living and dying, sanity and madness, from the point of view of an actress whose true reality

232

was the illusion of the stage not 'real life'; and a sufferer from mental illness whose 'madness' seemed to her the truest form of sanity. She explored the nature of art and life from many different points on the Wheel of awareness— sometimes reaching directly across it to the other side as fearlessly as she had tackled her roles when alive.

She also made it clear in the first interview exactly what her reasons for communication were. She needed, she said, to understand more about the purpose of her life, what it had been for. She needed, she said, to try to find answers—and the whole nature of the material she gave me appeared to bear this statement out.

At the end she summed up the message she wanted to leave as a result of her introspective journey. '**There is more**', she assured me, meaning that there was further significant progress and development for the soul beyond physical death. Many accounts of Near Death Experiences, as well as some religions, describe how each soul is subjected to a comprehensive 'flashback', or over-all review of the individual's life on Earth before it can pass further. The material Vivien gave me for her book seemed to reflect this process of self-examination.

The books were complete in themselves, though they can both be read as illustrations of the concepts presented here. The fact that each volume was extremely individual and they were so different to each other, revealed to me how the spiritual quest can take the form of an epic journey that forces us beyond our known horizons into entirely fresh territories. The medium and the artist need to take on trust realities and verities, which even they might sometimes wonder are symptomatic of a descent into madness. I felt the work was stretching me far beyond any limits I had known before.

Because the material was so unusual I had to use all my literary skills, acquired over a lifetime of novel-writing, journalism and publishing, to make sense of the mass of information I was given and put it into readable form. Puzzling for months over fragments of 'dictation' that appeared to be in some undecipherable cipher, the excitement of cracking the code and unveiling the mystery carried both myself and the members of my original 'support team' —particularly Paul and Jaine, a friend who is also a medium—along like a surging tide.

Though based on communications both with and from the two individuals who presented themselves to me in my capacity as a medium, the books are in a wider sense about communication with and from anyone who chooses to participate in the on-going quest for clarity and meaning—they encourage us to 'explore the threshold' by every means possible. Because death is not an 'end' but a change of focus, those who have experienced it can communicate from what they perceive as 'their' side of the 'Moonlit Door', even while they are continuing to progress; and mediumship being a two-way process, there are responsibilities on both sides. Those in Spirit may very much need our physical energy and assistance in order to help them explore their own thresholds.

When I first encountered this concept in my 'conversations' with Mist and with my 'angel in a grey suit'—that I might be able to use my strength and my energy in order to help and encourage them—I found it very disconcerting. But I reflected later that if my Guides were 'there for me', the fact that I was able to 'be there' for them—to whatever extent—was surely cause to face my own life with renewed resolve and courage. This brings its own sense of 'belonging', for though we travel separately, we are all travelling together on the same journey—the artist, the shaman, like the priestess or even the dead, all simply at different points on the Wheel.

The concept is not living or dying, this world or the next. As we will see, it by-passes the idea of life and death in offering a platform, a safe place to stand where those who have died can meet with the living, contributing and seeking answers, dealing with weaknesses, flaws and emotional baggage before moving on. There may be unfinished business, unresolved relationships on both sides. The problems of the dead reflect those of the living. Everyone meets as an equal, striving and progressing in his or her own way.

The statement from Rosemary Brown's communicating group of musicians appears to embody the same message that nearly all communicants from the world beyond have tried to make clear to the living—it is also inherent in most religious teachings and is implied in every message a medium receives from the 'Other Side'—that the soul does not die—that there is another life beyond this one, a life in spirit.

But both Bax and Vivien Leigh had further contributions to offer concerning this life, rather than any future existence. Creative artists of the highest caliber, they created new works of art in the books they gave me. Both have passed on, yet they are not dead; their artistry still burns, they are still contributing, not wanting the significance of what they learned on their life's journey to be lost. It appears that—as with the musicians who came to Rosemary Brown—creative artists can be so driven by their need to communicate and the conviction that their work will help mankind, they try to continue their 'explorations of the threshold' even after physical death.

In this sense Bax gave us joy in the physical, the ability to see life through his music; Vivien gave us vision to probe the distorting mirrors of the mind to reach the truth beyond.

When I set to work on the first of the three books I had been assigned—and even after I had completed the first two—I had no real idea of what the 'bigger picture' behind the whole undertaking might be. Even when struggling with the early drafts of this manuscript, I was frustrated by the fact that there did not seem to be any point to the three books in a collective sense—yet I was certain there must be. I intuitively knew there was a third book, and that it would be about me and my work as a medium—in some way this would underpin or clarify the first two. But the task was hugely difficult and took much longer to complete.

I began work on 'the third book' immediately after *A Season with Vivien Leigh* was safely published, jotting down random thoughts and notes as they occurred to me, trying out different formats and discarding them. Over the next five years I wrote and rewrote the whole text some five or six times but still could not get it right.

Late in 2010 I hit on the idea of using the

twenty-two cards of the Major Arcana as a framework and various pivotal thoughts seemed to come together. But the title and sub-title continued to change over the months. Originally this book was to be called *Knocking on the Moonlit Door: A Medium's Tale*; it evolved into *Maverick Medium: Working with Spirit*. I went through so many 'false starts' as to the presentation of this third book that I wondered at one point whether I would (or should) be working (as I had originally intuited) with another collaborator in spirit. No-one, however, seemed to present themselves as a possible third partner in the venture in this sense.

I hit on the idea of perhaps having the third book presented by a kind of Editor-in-Spirit—someone who, like Bax and Miss Leigh, had already passed over and would know what they were talking about. It was a crazy idea, but I envisioned that if I made myself available and left the channels of mediumship open, a suitable communicator might present him- or herself. I had felt throughout that many departed spirits who had been prominent in the arts had also been involved and were offering their support, however peripherally—so with this in mind, I anticipated some departed literary figure or even an editor in life might make an appearance.

Sure enough, a presence did emerge. The image I received was a 'snapshot' of a young

238

woman with what seemed to be a pale or white beret slanted on the side of her head over her long hair, and prominently vivid lipstick. I identified the image (after some investigation) as the poet Sylvia Plath, discovering the actual black-and-white portrait image I had 'seen' and finding that the appearance of the slanted beret on her hair was actually a pale patch of reflected light.

However, I was reluctant to accept this—particularly as Sylvia Plath, an amazingly gifted poet, had committed suicide. But I did receive the following composition—from her or from some other source—though she did not remain in communication after I had identified her picture and I continued to work on alone.

I am the Moonlit Door

All meet
AT THE MOONLIT DOOR,
FROM EITHER SIDE,
VOICES FROM HERE AND BEYOND.

Which is here? This side or the other side?
A door is open, empty, nothing, air.
Spiders webs woven fresh each day, the only barrier.
It is nothing. The only thing that defines it is the frame, the boundary.

For the suicide, it is the square of the gas oven.
For the tired soul the grill of the confessional

Fragments of sound from those who have passed this way
Snatches, glimpses.

No definition, only by removing the defining elements.
The door is the way, the threshold, but it leads to nowhere but the other side, which in its turn leads to this side.
Does it exist? Can it exist?
Transcending existence, what lies beyond that?
The door does nothing.
It says nothing.
It is nothing.
It is not there, cannot be there,
There is no being.

So what to make of it?
Here at the door, we—they—?

Whether you describe yourself as a poet, a composer, an artist, a medium, the truth is that there is no definition of the state of being which has been summarized as 'knocking on the moonlit door'.

We do not choose to be there and knock, but we have no choice. The way has brought us here, the door lies ahead. Behind us there is darkness, the path we have trodden to get here. What would be the point of going back? We know there is nothing there.

Moonlight. Shadow. Illusion. No colour. No defining points. Which the shadow, which the light?

Is there anybody there? we ask.
Is there anybody there? they ask.

I am the moonlit door.

12

THIS ROUGH MAGIC: SPEAKING FOR BAX

'It's always a fight for an original writer because any original writer will always force the world to see the world his way. The people who don't want to see the world your way will always be angry.'

Joe Orton

Writing the Bax book opened up the world for me in ways I could never have dreamed of. I was determined to do my best for him, and for his sake I dared to contact hugely eminent individuals in the world of music and entertainment.

The opera and ballet impresario Ellen Kent agreed to write a Foreword. Then I happened to be interviewing one of the most brilliant pianists of our time, David Owen Norris, on the phone for the magazine of which I was Arts Editor. I had never met him, but when I mentioned our book launch he offered out of the blue not only to attend but to play two of Bax's piano pieces—*May Night in the Ukraine* and *Gopak*. It was an amazingly gracious gesture. We also invited a Bax orchestrator, Graham Parlett, and after the launch held

242

a small reception where Paul and I found ourselves discussing Bax, music, the nature of genius and art in general in highly illustrious and stimulating company.

An actor friend, George Telfer, had also been present at the launch to read some of Bax's words from the book, while I had talked about it as best I could, giving an introduction to the work and how it had come to be written. The audience had responded favourably, we thought, but the following day I felt compelled to start noting down my feelings and impressions after we had read the review of our event.

1 AFTER THE REVIEW

Apart from unstinting praise for David and George—deservedly, and good for them, I'm glad they got something out of it all—the review hurt a bit, because what I'd said had been taken out of context. Also, inevitably I suppose, we had been largely judged on my own nervous and stumbling efforts to try and communicate the wonder—power—richness— of Bax's prose. I'd obviously been charitably dismissed as an elderly, though well-meaning crank.

I hadn't wanted to talk about the mediumship aspect or how the book had been achieved, but had to raise two points likely to be asked—again inevitably—at any event like this: *Do you really believe in all this mumbo-jumbo? And WHY ME?* Result in the review: 'She explained how Sir Arnold had come to her in trance'—UGGGGGGGHHHH!!!!!

The reviewer reported he *'enjoyed the music very much and will certainly seek out Bax in the future.'* BUT—there had to be one, of course— *'He found Bax's words conveying meanings to be interpreted by the listener, much like horoscopes'.* Though he *'enjoyed the imagery of the patterns of music to be found in the tips of seagull's wings and footsteps in the snow',* he *'had the nagging feeling he had heard them somewhere before.'*

He might have allowed his slightly barbed comments, which gave the end a distinct sting in the tail, to be laced with—tolerance? compassion, even—but instead there was a distinct Fringe spikiness in:

'Understandably Dilys is often questioned on the validity of her communications with the spirit world. She is of the opinion that true artists must possess a spirituality that means they don't need to ask these questions. Your reviewer is clearly no artist then.'

Even though my whole life has been spent in trying to find the best way to put across what I have to say, I realized again—perhaps with a kind of sad finality, this time—how absolutely impossible true communication is.

244

What I'd actually said was that I considered true artists—those who matter, those whose work matters and will matter in a hundred years from now—to have a spiritual dimension which means they don't question where inspiration comes from or how the result is achieved. Even that was a clumsy thing to say—but how else can you put it?

David's playing was described as *'quite exquisite performance of two of Bax's pieces by David Owen Norris'* ('the most interesting pianist in the world', please!!) and George *'no stranger to Fringers'* was praised for *'his readings of (Bax's) thoughts from the other side'* (excuse me while I cringe): *'—his delivery was everything we have come to expect from his Gielgud and Burton.'* Well done George, hope you can use that review somewhere.

I was a bit deflated. But sitting afterwards in the Palace Hotel listening to a concert by bassoonists (another event in that year's Buxton Music Festival) I had a revelation that was the true start, if you like, of my/our journey. As well as the review, the Polaroid pictures we had taken on the morning of the launch, of Paul and me standing outside the Old Hall (the venue where we held the launch), had deflated me a bit too. I look like a squat, solid elderly woman. No sign of the figure inside, the slim and chic Arts Editor, acclaimed author, TV & recording personality who can hold her own on late-night chat shows with other erudite and fascinating figures from literature.

IT WILL NEVER HAPPEN. But suddenly, I got enlightened, as they say. Bax felt just like me. He too must have cringed inside when he saw articles written about him like the one we had just seen in an old copy of the *Picture Post* (purchased by Graham Parlett at the Antiques Fair, which was also on in Buxton that weekend)—those ghastly images that tried to make a tubby, elderly man with thinning hair look glamorous—and on a page that had the lithesome figures of Fred and Ginger dancing across the opposite one. How it must have hurt him.

I've just been shown more about my task, how hard it's going to be to speak for him. How I'm going to have to take the knocks personally as we take the book forward and its ripples (hopefully) widen. People will not judge it as my work, or even Paul's (he *'talked of his research'* is all the space the reviewer gave him). They won't get to the heart of what has been said, because they will be far too concerned on establishing a mental superiority, wasting time on discussing my credentials, whether it's cranky because I am a medium, whether the book should have been written at all—

246

But isn't this what our task is all about? Isn't this why Bax needs someone to go with him to the edge of the world? Even my training and years of discipline as a medium were needed to get here, and now, this is the great adventure. For him and me, for us all.

We're alike, him and me, both ancient and doddering has-beens whose souls are still young and beautiful—to us, anyway—but who are aware of the frustrations of communicating this youth and beauty to others.

He soon put me right about the review, gave me once more his fresh take on seeming reality.

Interpretation by the listener is not necessarily the province only of horoscopes of the modern-day kind, regarded as entertainment and as such derided. Horoscopes were the powerful revelations of hugely skilled adepts, revealing innate truths which the seeker could wisely use or else refuse, in his folly, to hear.

The ancient oracles all spoke in riddles. All art is given on many levels, or else the rigidity of the framework would mean it collapsed under the weight of trying to be so explicit that it addressed the needs of millions in intimate detail. Only the foolish deny the essential formlessness of artistic communication, that it is a quest and a progression, not a finite point made.

As communicator, interpreter for him, I have to take the knocks because he cannot. So though it's frustrating for me and will likely be hurtful, this is the job I've been asked to do. It's not an easy job. It takes all my skills as a medium, translator of his words and presenter for him. All my skills as a writer, a communicator of words. Even, perhaps, my apprentice training in the Mysteries.

Rough, certainly, and I have a suspicion it will get rougher. But magic, oh yes. True Magick of the highest order.

Notes:
- The quote about 'Nothing that has not been heard somewhere else'. Well, there can never be any completely original, fresh truth that has never been heard before—only different stages of revelation to different individuals.
- Pioneers are always breaking new ground—discovering different ways of communicating. Innovators all suffer, but it doesn't matter what kind of mess you get into, as someone said—*so long as you're read*. The suffering is part of the experience.

248

2 THE MUSIC OF ARNOLD BAX

Bax was a medium too. He had that link with nature, from birth. Music to him was the same as breathing—it was a vocation. The image he gave me was Prospero in *The Tempest*—a magician, a shaman, a magus. Even the words of the play sound like spells:

> *The wild waves whist*
> *The isle is full of noises*
> *Brave new world*
> *This rough magic*

I was given a line of poetry....sea...haunted landscape? I discovered that it was by Yeats: *'that dolphin-torn, that gong tormented sea'*— from the poem *Byzantium.* You can hear the music as you speak it.

Without knowing the poem you see the line as music and Bax was using it to help illustrate how his music sees music beyond music. The essential music is everywhere—whether you call it Truth or God or whatever—and you can only approach it through a kind of filter (i.e. by using the piano keys or through written notes on the musical staves.)

Bax probably experienced the trance state where one is in touch with this kind of thing, all the time. It was as natural to him as breathing—the 'inspiration' we discussed. Coleridge, Poe and others achieved the trance-like state, the altered consciousness through drugs but Bax could do it without that.

His music shows that it isn't necessary to tear yourself apart as they did, in order to create art. They got it through the shamanic 'tearing apart by demons'. His music has these dark depths and dimensions too, and makes comments on the subject but without subjecting the listeners to the horrors. He actually shows you through easy ways how to turn the pain and suffering of living onto its head. The natural elements work in his music easily. He has got the powers; but they are so subtle you don't notice them.

This is 'synesthesia'—a state where some or all the senses are working together. Some people can 'hear' colour or 'see' sound. His vision was beyond all of them. You can go a little or a lot into his music, his vision. He never lost touch with generally accepted 'reality' as they did. His music is both limitless yet constrained. He was aware of both the structural form and the limitlessness of the powers. Compare Prospero's speeches: *'I have summoned spirits from the mighty deep, I have done this, I have done that.'*

You could relate Bax to Coleridge, Poe, Pink Floyd. He has no time, no fashion. Like Shakespeare, he is Everyman, every age. And the tree shape he described to me (like the branches of an espaliered tree being trained horizontally against a wall)—those layers of growth are the multi-layered structure of what he has to say. In every age, like Shakespeare, he can comment relevantly on the age. Shakespeare only used a small vocabulary. Bax did the same. You have to see him out of his context, like Shakespeare, to get the full picture of what his art achieves. Like a natural force. Nobody knows how Shakespeare wrote his plays, so nobody knows how Bax wrote his compositions. Not like Mozart—like lightning striking.

*   *   *

The 'Dinas' Concept

'It has given me great happiness to feel that people still remember, still think of me and still understand, well, that I am very much alive, you know, it is wonderful because some people, they have no realization of life after death. They think when you are dead, you are dead.'
Spirit of Rudolph Valentino
(Speaking through the mediumship of Leslie Flint)

'The trouble with dying is that you become dismissed as "dead".'
Spirit of Sir Arnold Bax
(Speaking through the medumship of Dilys Gater in Summer with Bax)

251

It is a well-known fact that spiritual work proceeds in a completely different manner to factual learning or scientific investigation—if anything, it works backwards. So far as psychic or mediumship ability is concerned, the understanding of the gifts and the capability to accept them in their entirety is what most commonly stands in the way. The philosopher Descartes said: 'I think, therefore I am' but the psychic or medium needs to turn this method of approach on its head. His standpoint must be: 'I have done it, it is done: therefore though I might not understand how it happened or even believe that it is possible, I have proved by doing it that it can be done and that I am able to do it.'

This is what has happened with my three books. As I reach the eventual end of this—the third—I can at last understand how and why the other two had had to be written first. They have to be there in order to illustrate how the concept of communication that I am using actually works. I have written many books as 'a writer'—starting at the beginning and going on to the end. But this time Spirit wanted to start at the end—with the evidence—and then work backwards to show how it had been achieved. I had to know I could do it before I found out what I had done, as it were.

Through the existence of the books themselves, we have proof that these communications can be made, we see it to be achievable and possible; they illustrate that we can all approach from different points on the circle or Wheel, wherever we are, whether 'dead' or 'living', to talk together.

When Spirit gave me the task of producing the books I was also given a concept to illustrate what I had undertaken. Once again it was my Celtic ancestry that providing the image to work with. I was brought back to Wales, the green landscapes of mountains and waters I had walked as a novice in the Mysteries, speaking to me in language I can only now begin to understand—familiar yet powerfully strange; lovely yet mysterious; reassuring yet opening doors onto infinity.

I call these the *Dinas (pronounced* deenass*)* books—communications achieved in 'the between place', the *Dinas*. The word *Dinas* as it is used here represents a 'state of mind' where artists and thinkers from all dimensions can meet to share thought and experience. In this sense the term *Dinas* signifies a place of discussion, an opportunity for communication between all who can enter 'the between place' and benefit from the exchange. It is a stopping place not for those wanting to be convinced but for minds already actively searching and prepared to participate in an on-going journey.

The word *Dinas* is Welsh, meaning 'city', but it can be translated simply as 'The Place'. Often it was the fortified 'place', fort, castle or headquarters of the prince or chief. Essentially, it was a central point, a meeting place, a place for communicating, for discussion and negotiation.

The vision we each have of 'the place' will differ. I am Welsh, and to me 'the place' is the ancient, ruined outer bailey of some early Welsh castle in the wilds of Snowdonia. Amid cloud, mountain peak, lake and green hillside, a crumbling keep and three towers form the square of the fortress. The stone has sunk in the earth and is now barely visible, just an outline that marks the gathering-place of the leader. Here he called his people together, and here they gravitated at times of danger, or when their way of life was threatened by invasion or annihilation. They came for safety and counsel to this place where they could lick their wounds, re-establish their identity and make their plans.

The *Dinas* provides a safe haven, opportunity to reflect, to take counsel; here the wisdom of experience can be weighed against the impetuosity of youth. Others will of course see 'the place' differently—maybe not even as a place at all. It is also a concept— of aspiration, of the heart's desire, the tarot

254

Ace of Cups, the unattainable Holy Grail of Arthurian legend: it is the secret magic of Merlin, the core of wisdom and truth revealed. Achieving or entering 'the place' is in fact more than a physical decision to act, it is a state of mind, a time, an energy.

These definitions from the Mini Oxford Dictionary will help to clarify the many aspects we can consider in our identification of 'the place':

Court—n.
1 Space enclosed by walls or buildings... enclosed quadrangle open or covered
2 Sovereign's residence; his establishment and retinue; the body of courtiers; sovereign and his retinue as ruling power
3 Formal assembly held by sovereign at his residence
4 ...Assembly of judges or other persons acting as tribunal to hear and determine any cause; place in which justice is administered
5 (Meeting of) qualified members of company or corporation...
6 Attention paid to one whose favour, affection or interest is sought

The original *Dinas* concept as it presented itself to me in the early years of working on these books, seemed to concern the way to find or reach 'the place': and to discover what the significance of the *Dinas* or 'place' might be. As we have discussed earlier—why meet or communicate at all?

As a place of gathering, it is a place to aspire to, but not necessarily to stay beyond a certain time. You then go on—so there is a journey in progress both before (to get there) and after (when you leave).

The Court, as we see from the definitions above, is also a collective, not an individual thing. It is a meeting together of different people, 'courtiers' or members who in their different ways all participate and contribute. There is a drawing together of threads here, an interweaving.

The nature of this concept reveals that whatever ideas might be found or included, however original (which it must be in order to present a fresh thought or view) is also influenced, overshadowed. In art, originality cannot help but be coloured with the outside influences that have shaped it. So the individual, the artist or spiritual traveller is alone yet does not—and cannot—exist mentally in isolation, even though that person may want to remove himself or herself physically from others.

The Tower

'The Tower...is ruled by Mars...
(Its windows) denote a narrow view of the world.
The card reflects

that nothing can stand against the will of the divine.'

Jonathan Dee

The image of a ruined castle keep or tower—my vision of 'the *Dinas* place'—is another of those archetypal symbols that have huge significance beyond the literal. Dark Towers have figured very largely in literature and the words themselves give us a sense of brooding timelessness, possible historic links, fallen power of the heroic kind—these are places where worlds meet, where mysterious, even magical events are likely to occur, where anything might happen.

From my own point of view, I was fascinated to realize that my initial identification of 'the place' as a lost, abandoned ruin set in the high mountains of North Wales, surrounded by clouds, lakes and intractable rocky peaks had a deeper significance than I had at first thought. The pagan Celts who lived there led semi-nomadic lifestyles, pasturing their flocks in the summer, retreating to the friendlier lowlands for the harsh and bitter winter. As warriors too, they were continually prepared for the guerilla warfare that meant they could not settle for any length of time.

It comes as something of a revelation that there were no large Celtic cities or even towns in Wales. The centres of the people's stability and security were the towers and

257

keeps of castles built by their princes and war-
lords. *'Dinas'*, meaning The Fortified Place, is
portrayed in my vision as in crisis, in ruin. The
card known as The Tower in the tarot pack
is often described as 'The Tower Struck by
Lightning' or 'The Falling Tower'. It signifies
huge social upheaval, great change, apparent
disaster. But it also reminds us that seeming
disaster can sometimes be a force for good;
troubles can 'make or break' the human spirit,
temper it in the fire so it emerges stronger and
wiser. We can come through trying times of
change—the ruins can be rebuilt to a fresher,
newer vision.

'Dear ones of earth, we do not expect miracles
from you, but we do say,
obey the highest urge in your thoughts and in
your life.'

White Eagle

'When I was on the edge of the world, then
yes, I understood all in a flash of lightning or a
crash of thunder. It all came and I tried to put
this into my work… I tried to put the knowledge
into what I wrote down but it's very, very much
of an echo…….

'We all tried in our way. I personally have always travelled alone.
One can talk to others about the experience—
one can exchange experiences,
but how do we know—how did I know—whether
another artist had travelled to the same edge of
the world that I had? The more you exchange
experiences with others, the less sure you become
that they understand what you are saying. The
more artists come together and discuss their
work and their vision, the more one becomes
aware that those visions are very disparate.

'If one has seen an angel, the angel may be
the same angel, and yet take a different form.
Everything is very much to do with my own
journey, my own travelling alone, and no-one
could come with me.'

Sir Arnold Bax
(Through the mediumship of Dilys Gater in
Summer with Bax)

13
THE MESSAGE

'What was it all about?
.....I want you to know that there is more.'
Vivien Leigh
(Through the mediumship of Dilys Gater—A
Season with Vivien Leigh)

One of the most wonderful aspects of mediumship for me is the sense of 'living' my communication with another person, being invited to their mind, entering into their experience. This awareness of sharing, passing concepts and impulses from mind to mind as simply and easily as possible, was very marked as I worked on the Dinas *manuscripts.*

While I was still editing the 'Vivien Leigh book', Paul and I held a discussion with our friend Jaine, who is also a medium. We recorded it as a reference to the way the material was progressing. The following, taken from the transcriptions, gives some idea of the thrilling, energizing atmosphere in which we were working. (Editorial comments on the text are given in brackets),

Dilys: I had done everything in the psychic books to find the answers. There seemed to be no way forward. So I prayed for answers...For someone to guide me...And then when Bax came through he showed us there was another way of looking at things...

We had been in contact with someone musical before. I had made brief contact with Beethoven—but we never thought of asking him. Then there was that time I met Mozart—the man I thought had been Mozart in the past—(*DG: The case is detailed in my book* Past Lives). Strangely, Beethoven wouldn't have been satisfactory, so I suggested we contact Bax. We had also contacted him before, very briefly. Paul didn't want to listen to what he said then, but Bax did say some very interesting things about texture, and talked about rain on water, which we lost—so I said, this time we must tape it...

Jaine: I knew right from the start that it wasn't your voice (*DG: When she listened to the tapes of the Bax communications*)—it was completely different, completely different thoughts, so intelligent—just so clear, amazing thoughts and such a different take on life. I wondered how you were doing it from a point of mediumship, how you were getting the words and whether you were getting impressions or pictures in your mind as well.

(*DG: Though I had never thought of it myself before, Jaine pointed out the similarity to*

261

translating from a foreign language.)

Jaine: When I listened to the tape of the trance, you chose your words so carefully. You also mentioned the impressions that had come into your mind, and that you had to decide which words Bax meant, so it was like translating from his thoughts.

Dilys: At the start of the venture, we didn't know it would turn out to be a book. Around the actual sessions though, there was a lot of discussion, Paul and I talking around what came through for weeks. Other ideas and perceptions and realizations kept coming. They *(ie: Bax and Vivien Leigh)* put in other contributions in images, ideas, pointers. You wonder when you are doing this whether it's just chance, as it might appear to other people, synchronicity. Or if it's real. The same thing happened with Vivien Leigh, I described how I was 'open' all the time to what might be going on and found this drained me far more than it used to when I was doing any other kind of mediumship. It almost takes you away from being able to cope with real life, because you're permanently on an 'open channel'.

With Bax it was apparent from the start that there was some kind of agenda. Bax kept suggesting (the) different meeting places—in mental pictures—though we weren't sure where they were. I even wondered whether the

262

places he gave me were just my imagination. I had no idea they were real locales until much later: I had asked Paul not to discuss his research with me. *(DG: Paul, as co-author of* Summer With Bax, *provided all the chapters of biographical detail and notes)*

Dilys: Each time Bax and I would meet in some specific place, but with Vivien Leigh the process was different.

(DG: Miss Leigh 'presented' herself visually as has been described, standing in dim light in falling snow at the ornate gates of a graveyard with high columns and looming gravestones beyond. This turned out to be a stage 'set' rather than a 'real' place.)

Dilys: ...She has been in the same place all along, we've met up or connected at the gates of the cemetery. She has never moved from that spot, though she has made herself far more flexible. She seems to have let go of the physical, whereas Bax was very close to the physical. Every time I met up with him, it was somewhere physical, talking to him.

I never got the impression Bax was a spirit, he is a real, physical person, and you also get that sense of the world, which he loved so much. He's not talking about any other world, he's talking about this world.

Jaine: What I found absolutely incredible—knowing very little about classical music, or the composers or the whole subject—was the way he saw life as music. It was completely and utterly in his mind—seeing the seagull with the dark-tipped feathers, for example—the footprints in the snow. Everything was notes in his mind.—And it was so different, it was nothing to do with your mind, Dilys.

It was as though everything was loved and loving, everything was connected with.

Dilys: I was very struck by how he seemed to love the world too—he said so himself—but when he used the word love, he was talking of levels, subtleties of love. He sees everything as a composition, a part of the whole.

So his music is expressing a feeling, as though his art is an inspiration, his inspiration an expression of a love of everything. Might this be the nature of all art? You could say an artist doesn't always like the world or the people in it, but there is always that sense of connection—whatever the artist feels connected to. I recognize Bax as a genius, a greater genius than has previously been appreciated because through this work I came to know his mind so well.

There was no-one who didn't like him—in Paul's research we haven't come across anyone, a single person who ever said a bad word about him, even after he died. He seems to have had an essential core—like his music—of truth, honesty, goodness. All artists must have it to some extent, even though often in their private lives they are objectionable because they have to defend themselves against the world. Vivien Leigh had this very noticeably in her communications—it shone through, a kind of innate honesty and truthfulness.

There is a connection present with something higher or bigger than oneself, whether this is called creativity or inspiration. This is the nature of inspiration, where it comes from and what it does. Bax obviously felt it was something that connected him and the music to the earth, because his music is quite connected to the earth. After all, he did say 'Don't ask me about music, it's all the same—whether it's the music of the spheres—or whatever—that you're juggling with—'. So in a way, it's so simple. The way Bax looks at it, it's so simple.

Inspiration and Genius: The Artist's View

Jaine: In *Farewell My Youth (his autobiography)* Bax describes standing on a bridge in Ireland, seeing the water falling, for an instant he was the earth, the water, the atmosphere, all of it. That total connection. I think he probably had that sense of connection a lot.

Dilys: Probably something that was natural to him, that he mightn't have been able to describe. Universal. He talks about being in the void, suspended. If you are getting that kind of trance-like state, water falling is something that can induce it. He was probably going into trances of some kind, getting insights all the time, often without knowing about it.

Jaine: When he was composing—. A different state of mind.

Dilys: His footprints in the snow, the notes—in a way, just being aware of that is putting you into a different mind-set, isn't it?

Jaine: Also, really living in the moment. He's seeing things as they are. Really, absolutely seeing.

Dilys: Maybe the inspiration, the genius, is that ability to see what's there, just to see things.

Jaine: Did he say time was slower, strange sometimes?

Dilys: He talked about it not existing—'Neither alive nor dead'. Vivien Leigh did the same, she is in a kind of 'dressing room' between living and dying, between 'performances'. She is more aware than Bax, who only sees the golden sea and does not relate to what happens after. He's still tied to living

(DG: My vision of where Bax might be, where he was speaking from, is of a small boat gently rocking on a sea golden with sunset light. He mentioned in the last session that he sees love as 'a golden sea' into which one can sink and drown. We discovered later that he spent part of his last day standing on the Atlantic coast watching the sun go down over the sea in the west.)

Jaine: The moments he saw, they were so vivid—universal, totally.

Dilys: We can see that kind of altered consciousness on different levels as well. There's a conscious level where you do it—he sat down to compose—. But Elgar plucking the notes out of the atmosphere, that's a different kind of mind-set. Bax says he doesn't do that, but he talks about translating, how he got the image—but how can you tell, if you feel the thing as say the sea, how can you choose which

267

wave? He must have been very well aware of the structure, of using the structure in some way. You couldn't comment on it if you were not aware of the process.

Dilys: I have felt almost from the beginning that there were three people turning up—Now Vivien Leigh is so different (to Bax) but in her way, I think she is doing something similar. They are two people who don't seem to have wanted to progress further yet. So they've got what you call unfinished business of some sort, both for their own satisfaction. I think Bax particularly feels as he must have felt when he travelled about.

I think he had that great awareness of need, of people's need, and he's trying in some way to maybe offer help—because he does give you such a huge positive boost, purely from being himself, and helping you to see through his eyes. So in a way, he's saying, 'Well walk with me a bit, and I'll show you how I see it'. That's what he said in the interviews: 'I'll tell you what I saw, what it was like for me'.

Now he's saying 'Let's walk together a bit further, and you can see a bit more of what it was like for me'... It's given us a complete lift through what has been a very bad winter after that summer we spent working with him. It's really, really been something that has kept us going through a very tough, depressing time, when you're lost and don't know which way to go. He's really saying, 'Let's walk a bit, and I'll talk to you a bit'.

Paul: In the beginning of January, *(ie: 2006, the year the book was published)* when we were waiting for the copies to arrive from the printers, we sat here and Dilys said 'I wonder if we're doing the right thing—'.

Dilys: Well, it's all done in faith.

Paul:—And she said: 'What's the reaction going to be from the people who know about him, particularly on the Sir Arnold Bax website—the musicians, the Bax authorities—.' (She was) Very dubious, quite fearful.

Jaine: But the whole thing is about inspiration, and the book, as it is, is quite an amazing book anyway. The knowledge—the humanity—it's extraordinary as a piece of work, and it seems that the musical world is opening up to it as a piece of extraordinary work as much as anything. *(DG: By this time the book had received some favourable reviews.)*

Dilys: I think as we go on, we might find with Vivien Leigh that there's an awful lot of coming and going. I have had a contribution from the third person since—. I wondered

269

why there were three—I don't know—it's not anything so specially meaningful—they were working together, I think—but each separate—because what I found was, Bax gave us a wonderful lift, and the encouragement to go on—and it was worth going on. Vivien Leigh came with problems (*DG*: *Her Bipolar Disorder*) and she showed me the world turned on its head—I mean, she turned strength into weakness, and weakness into strength, and she's helped to put the balance right. She says—'Look at my case, consider what happened to me'.

(**DG:** The third communicator has made only one very brief contact so far. I glimpsed the most amazing and powerful sense of brilliant white light at a time when I was very much in need of reassurance, which lifted me beyond all fear and worry. Since I believe the third communicator is the strange magus Austin Osman Spare, this would make sense.

I was rather dreading having to venture into his world of 'chaos magic' with its nihilistic overtones, but this one contact revealed that if and when he does choose to communicate, the messages will come from 'beyond chaos', beyond the darkness, from the source of that wonderful, unbelievable brightness.)

Is There a Purpose?

Dilys: I think I always felt that Bax was there. Paul didn't want to listen the first time, but what Bax had to say was extremely relevant. He was there, he was available and seemed to know what he was talking about. So I got on very well the first time we made contact. I wasn't trying to get anything out of him.

The first time was where I saw him in the room—sitting in the room I've described in the country house and (I had an image of) Paul seeming to go into the room dressed in tennis flannels, like a young man in the 1930s, he got told off, and went out again. So this time, when we decided to contact him, I focused on the room and the name. Then I got the image I've described of all this rain on the sea, on water. It all seems a bit easier when you look back and say 'this happened' or 'that happened', because you can see what the result was, but at the time, you don't really know what you're doing.

I was always conscious of Bax being there, and always conscious of him being a person. *(DG: I still feel him around.)*

Jaine: So effectively, Bax decided that he was going to communicate through you as a

271

couple, that you're the right medium, Dilys, and you're right, Paul, because you know about the music. So you kind of got chosen by him, rather than you choosing him.

Dilys: Maybe when we made contact that first time, he was giving us some kind of an interview, a test—but Paul didn't think so. He went in, as it were, and sat down—the golden boy in his flannels—'Now come on sir, I need to put my literary career in order—how would you tackle it?' And Bax says: 'How dare you, young man. Who do you think you're talking to? Go off and learn some respect.'

Jaine: You didn't have any agenda, did you?

Dilys: Well, no. But this time, we did get a way to go.

Jaine: Even though this time there was no agenda either.

Dilys: I was written out. I didn't know what to do at this point. Was there any other way? We were trying to go to an authority, as it were. We were trying to go to an artist, a great person who would teach us—.

Jaine: Like a mentor?

Dilys: Yes, because I felt that I had gone as

far as I could go, and there was no-one else to ask. Not a 'Spirit Guide' type of thing—*(DG: I knew this was different to my work with Mist.)*

Jaine: Don't you think though, that the way it's worked out, though this has happened for you, Bax has had his own agenda?

Dilys: I think he has.

Jaine: He's actually wanted to say certain things, put certain things over. And although you—we—have all learned a lot already, it's still going on.

Dilys: Yes, he's still there and this is why I get so tired, because although he's not 'communicating' in so many words—as in the conversations—everything I talk about regarding the contents of the book is still a part of it. It's as though I'm inside his head, and when you're in somebody's head, you start to think or see things the way they are looking at them.

* * *

Explorers

The years of working with Bax and Miss Leigh on their books, of writing and rewriting this third volume so that it is not only readable

273

but actually makes some sense, of following the fragmentary dictates by which Spirit clarified my thought processes—all these have brought me, as I said, in a full circle. Now I have reached the castle ruins in the mist—'the *Dinas* Place', the threshold. And I am back in the mountains of Wales, where I started my spiritual journey as a girl.

I felt very strongly that there was some overall meaning to this work Spirit had asked me to do, but stumbled around for years trying to identify what it was. And now, having reached this point in the third book—'my' book, the one that, I eagerly anticipated, would clarify everything—I can see that there is no actual meaning as such, no 'end' as it were. Instead I am finding new ways to go, moving out of time and place. The journey has turned into an exploration—as it does for all the other travellers who pass this way, the painters, dancers, writers, performers and interpreters of their various arts—of this place between on which we all stand.

Using my mediumship, Bax and Miss Leigh—as well as other spirits who lent their energy and expertise to the venture—have been able to express their thoughts and opinions in a manner which, in accordance with their work in life, offers a commentary on the state of the world and of humanity. Both in their different ways were heroic travellers who loved life and valued their years of physical

274

living, both fully embraced the passions, the ecstatic joys and terrible frustrations of loving and trying to express that love in terms of their art.

A commentator said of Bax that because he was afraid of growing old, his music never fully matured into acceptance of old age—in other words he was never able to portray the dignity and gravitas of ageing in the way other artists have portrayed it. Vivien Leigh, on the other hand, fearlessly explored the loss of youth and beauty—particularly relevant to herself as one of the most beautiful women of her day—in her later films *The Roman Spring of Mrs Stone* and *Ship of Fools*.

I have said that I did not ask questions, simply took what Spirit gave and tried to make a good job of it. I could not see what these two communicators had in common—or, if they had nothing in common, why they had both appeared to dictate their books to me—literally until this point. Now I appreciate that they were both hugely gifted individuals—one could even use the word genius here, I think—who, when they passed over, still retained the passion and the questing spirit of youth. They came to me to continue, in effect, what they had been trying to complete in life.

They are still questioning, still exploring. No thought, no striving, no attempt to express what cannot be expressed in earthly terms is ever lost. That is the wonderful message of the

Dinas communications.

For me the message has also underlined the fact that whatever evidence may be given, whatever miracles may be performed, whatever the spiritual world may give us, still this world—in general—is not disposed to listen or to learn.

Even more revelatory to me than the books themselves was the way in which my two eminent subjects were treated. I began to be aware after the launch of the Bax book (as I have mentioned earlier) that I was in effect 'standing in' for the composer and 'taking the flak' (as he might have put it) on his behalf. We have already agreed that visionaries, like prophets, are likely to be unappreciated in their own countries, or even their own worlds.

As a realist I began to see—very much as Rosemary Brown had described—that the way would not be easy. Hostile criticism was the least I could expect since I 'claimed' (in journalistic jargon) to be working with very eminent historical figures—regarding *A Season with Vivien Leigh* though, I was still unprepared for the vitriolic violence this book has provoked in certain quarters— though compensatingly, it has had incredibly supportive responses from people who actually knew Vivien when she was alive.

It was only while working on this final draft

that I came across an old paperback copy of *Unfinished Symphonies* (originally published in 1971) and was hugely and gratefully encouraged by Rosemary Brown's comments on her own work. For in this kind of situation you are more than ever on your own; it is almost impossible to encounter anyone else who understands what you are doing. So it was a wonderful boost to discover another medium who had passed through experience similar to mine and had recorded it in the very words I might have written myself:

'... *when the music began to come through Liszt warned me that the work would mean a great deal of suffering for me—from ridicule, from jealousy, and from harsh scepticism. He said that people would try to exploit me, people would try to suppress the music, people would try to take command, and that people would belittle me. All sorts of hurtful things would happen.*

'*He was quite correct. All these things happened to me, but he also said that if I would go through with it, what I was doing could be of value to the world. And for that reason I agreed to undertake the work.*

'*But he did warn me, and I did have the choice...*'

*   *   *

277

'I've got such a lot of things I'd like to say, because I see things from such a different viewpoint now. I want to talk particularly about life and death because my life was death and my death was life, in a way. I spent a lot of my time in coffins—I was an actress who acted death a lot—and half-death. I was ill, they said, but which was real? Sometimes I was dead, I was in a coma, I was in a trance, I was in a something—but I don't know, or I didn't know then, which was which.

'Life and death are actually so similar, and love and death, and sex and death, and the body and the spirit—or call it whatever you like—they are very much the same thing that prompts you. You spend your life hurrying towards death. The thanatos, *which is the death-wish, is perhaps what propels you through life...'*

Vivien Leigh
(*Through Dilys's mediumship in* A Season with Vivien Leigh)

'Though the seas overflow and the rivers burst their banks yet many waters cannot quench us for we are indestructible and in our weakness is our strength. Upon our brows we carry the stars and the moons are beneath our feet. As the eternal rocks are a part of each other, so our handclasp will wear away only in aeons of winter rain and the droughts of summer. We are indivisible for there is no seam and the fabric was woven by one loom.

'We are a garden of flowers of which there are many blooms yet all are enclosed within the same high wall. We are the colours in a prism of light that all are different and dart their separate ways and can never meet or be the same and yet are part of the whole. We have died separately so that we may know what it is to live together.

'We shall go forward together and still the waters to make a path. We shall read the stones and place the patterns of the clouds and the rippling of the rivers together so that all will be clear. We shall open the gates.'

Dilys Gater
Channelled in The Notta Manuscripts

'It's just like magic, like an amazing magic trick, only better.'

Spirit of a woman describing her death to Dilys

14
THE NOVICE MEDIUM

Interview with Dilys Gater
**4 *Guidelines for Development
Alone or in a Class***

*'The physical and the spiritual are
complementary polarities of the totality of the All
that is...As in a hologram, the All is present in
each facet.'*

Kenneth Meadows
*Where Eagles Fly: A Shamanic Way to Inner
Wisdom*

In the past, working as a medium (or indeed
a psychic) was not just a case of setting up a
table in a Psychic Fair or two; such activity
was of huge magnitude and carried heavy
penalties, the 'summoning of spirits' regarded
throughout the ages as so dangerous and
prohibited it could be punishable by death.
Called 'necromancy', it was viewed as one of
the most dreadful of sins or crimes. Even now
I hear apologetic comments from people who
feel they must conceal their visit to a medium
because their partner/friends/workmates 'don't
believe in all this, you see'.

I wrote many of my books on psychic and spiritual subjects in answer to the questions I am asked by people who do not understand the nature of their experiences or gifts but have found no-one in whom they can confide. This is an area where nothing in our society prepares or informs you—there are no courses on mediumship in any educational syllabus, not even a realistic 'official policy' about the standing of psychics and mediums within the community.

Developing as a medium can only be done by the individual working with, and learning to trust Spirit and his Guides, but the notes in this chapter are intended to offer subjects for discussion or meditation, a summary of ways of working and brief guides for the beginner. Further information can be found in my other books or by contacting anecdotespublishing@btinternet.com

Prayer and Protection

- You should always open and close your working sessions with prayers and ask Spirit to protect you and guide you wisely, not forgetting to offer thanks for whatever you have been given, even if you think nothing has happened and you have received nothing. If the novice medium undertakes his work seriously, responsibly and humbly, asking for help in his own spiritual progress rather than for frivolous reasons or out of personal arrogance, he will be quite safe.

- A good rule of thumb to apply to any questionable situation of a 'spiritual' nature, however seemingly potentially beneficial is that the danger signs to watch for are violent extremes of any sort (even 'good' ones!) and disruptive or manic imbalance.
- Departed spirits or other entities—like living people—do not necessarily always tell the truth and appearances can be deceptive.

Keep a Spiritual Workbook and Record your Progress

- The novice must learn to stay focused—keeping a spiritual journal or daybook can be helpful here; and you need the same dedication for spiritual work that you would give to a highly specialised art. You must be prepared for the hours, days and years of labour that is unique to the creatively gifted person but with which the average individual will be completely unfamiliar.
- Training in development as a medium—ideally also in any other kind of psychic work—involves regular practice of the disciplines of relaxation and meditation. In my development classes I explain to students, some of whom are very intuitively gifted or highly trained in healing or other

therapies, why our continuous working at relaxation, meditation and concentration is necessary. Progress in any further psychic disciplines cannot proceed without them— until the student has some mastery over the body he or she is unlikely to be able to work with the power of the mind.

Do not make claims that cannot be substantiated

- I will never undertake any communication as a medium where the enquirer demands 'proof' or some other kind of 'evidence'. You do not make conditions or bargain with Spirit. You must always have respect for what you are granted and take whatever you are given in faith and gratitude.

Take your work seriously

- Though the medium is often treated these days as someone who cannot be taken seriously, the exact opposite is the case: people are afraid that the medium and what he or she is doing might prove to be very serious indeed. But they may not want to hear the truth, whether about themselves or anything else, preferring to live with delusions that are comforting and familiar.

283

Do everything you can to alleviate unease or fear in others

- The terms 'occult' and 'arcane' mean 'secret', 'hidden': it is this awareness of hidden power—however perceived—and the ignorance of the public (urged on by the media) that combine to cultivate the uneasy atmosphere we encounter so often today. The tarot cards are an example: many individuals are wary of them and regard them as 'wicked' or 'evil', whereas they are nothing but squares of stiffened paper holding in themselves no power at all. It is the arcane knowledge they represent and the ability of adepts using them to gain access to Spirit, to other worlds and dimensions, that is really scary, so one of the basic aims of any practitioner should always be to remove fear not to create it.

Unfortunately a long tradition of 'gipsy's warnings' of doom and gloom, veiled threats of curses and bad luck continues to be perpetuated by self-important, sad or sick individuals who enjoy terrifying the credulous. It is a heady temptation to hint at personal magical power not to be trifled with—regardless of whether those concerned have any or not—and history contains many accounts of supposed 'witches' or 'magicians' who met with torture or death.

On investigation, however, you find most cases involved ignorance goaded by religious intolerance and the lust for power—sometimes in the persecuted as well as persecutors.

The word 'glamour' which is often used about the theatre, means 'transforming', 'changing'. It is a sad comment on our times that media people—'celebrities'—are now the icons, the saints of secular religion and the recognized figures of hope and aspiration in today's society.

Act responsibly at all times

• What really frightens people is the idea of stepping into the unknown, abandoning the safe ground of physical reality and leaving oneself open to whatever might be 'out there'. Might one become invaded or possessed, novices ask fearfully. Could you get 'stuck' somewhere and not be able to come back? How do you tell the difference between a good spirit and a bad one?—or protect yourself against the unfamiliar powers of the dark? It is true that mediums sometimes have to cope with situations that are unpleasant or frightening. You are tapping into hugely powerful forces of energy and if turned against you the results can be devastating—being under 'psychic attack', for example, or having to deal with 'bad trips' in states of altered consciousness.

Shamanic initiation is described as 'being torn apart by demons'.

- Ignorance, while no excuse, needs to be handled carefully. Danger lies in 'messing about', treating the psychic/spiritual as a game, a 'bit of fun' instead of taking it seriously—the casual use of planchettes or Ouija boards provide examples.

Do not provoke other people

- Fear—also superstition, indoctrination, blind expectation and over-reaction with no rational basis—are closely linked to ignorance and may provoke violent responses. The obvious solution would be for those concerned to educate themselves, but if there is already a blind spot within the mind, panic, even violence can be triggered by a single emotive word. Any 'spiritual' hysteria or 'religious fervor' whether regarded as positive or negative, should be avoided; these are likely to provoke reactions of personal fear/shame/guilt out of all proportion to the situation.

Do not cultivate personal power

- If the individual continues to follow a personal agenda rather than allowing himself to be guided, it can be hazardous to work with psychic/spiritual energies: megalomaniacs and the intolerance of innumerable Establishment institutions of various kinds have demonstrated this throughout history. Spiritual power is neither good nor bad. It depends what the individual chooses to do with it and even 'good intentions' do not justify the ego assuming psychic/spiritual power and using it for personal motives.

How do you deal with sexuality?

- The Chinese ideogram for the word 'I' is a combination of the symbols for the Sun and the Moon and their alternating and complementary qualities, a combination of the Yang and the Yin. Most belief systems recognize the partnership of male and female deities. There is nothing to stop the medium enjoying sexual relationships in a physical sense.

- Sexuality plays a part in working magic. Initiates learn to access sexual energy— the animal power of the body—to be used when needed. Healing systems like Reiki recognize the importance of balance between all the energy points or chakras including the base. This poem expresses the process of transcendence from the physical to the spiritual:

LOVE
put out both my eyes
BLIND
I feel my way

Yet onward creep
And do not look behind
Though dark my fiercest day

All lost, no rest but in my grave,
All gone, hope spent. Breath taken,
Worms' food, fear's fool, by life itself forsaken
I die and wake to

LOVE

*   *   *

Always trust Spirit unconditionally

- A medium has to trust Spirit absolutely, learning from his increasing experience, remembering he is a 'channel' to be kept clear, not worrying whether what he gets is satisfactory or trying to evaluate what comes through. You will be told only what you need to know, not necessarily what you ask. You cannot crash in, initiating procedures or posing trivial questions, whether to your guides or individual spirits. You do only what is permitted and must always have respect for the worlds and the spirits with which you are working.

- Spirit never gives anyone more to deal with than they can manage at any given time. If the novice approaches his work seriously, responsibly and humbly in a spirit of respect and faith there will be nothing to fear but everyone involved—both medium and enquirer—should not forget that when working with Spirit one is in a sense entering a sacred place and behave accordingly.

Remember a medium is only a channel and do not take matters into your own hands

- Occasionally messages or other visions are received which are in the nature of prophetic precognition. Someone may 'see' that a plane crash or other disaster is about to happen and mediums are often asked: 'What should you do in such a case?' One of the basic rules of not only the medium/priestess but of the artist vision is that one simply passes on the message, the truth received. What action others may choose to take is up to them—and though efforts have been made in the past to act on precognitive visions of disasters, and so on, they have never proved viable. The medium's role is to provide comment, not to initiate or bring about change in a material sense.

Learn as much as you can about the work you do and learn from your experience

- Even a potential 'maverick' needs to learn the accepted rules before he can discard or break them—a precept that also applies to the creative artist. Consider the careful paintings of the Renaissance based on principles of anatomy, line and form—an artist must be familiar with them before his style can develop into something that seems chaotic such as Impressionism or Cubism. In music, even if a composer's work seems to have no rules this can only be perceived with reference to traditional musical form. You must first find the main highway before you can branch off from it and strike out on your own. Only then will you begin to discover your true identity and accept the unique path you are required to tread, the task you alone must undertake.

Remember you are there to serve Spirit, and Spirit always knows better than you do

- This is part of the responsibility of the gift and as the medium's ability increases, so does his feeling of reverence and respect. The greater the power the less need to demonstrate it, and any truly powerful being reveals himself or itself by 'being' not 'doing. Sometimes this is difficult to understand, and the medium must advise those who want to make contact that they have to accept whatever comes through— even if there seems to be no answer—and not try to dictate their wants. Spirit always provides what is needed, not necessarily what individuals think they need, and in such cases the medium's assistance in interpreting the answer (or apparent lack of any answer) can be crucial.

It is truth, and the acceptance of truth, which are the tools of the novice medium. The clairvoyant/shamanic vision, like the conditions of battle, strips away small petty details that do not matter and concentrates on the important ones. It provides an over-view stripped of artificial sentimentality and biased judgment— and if this horrifies the oversensitive soul, seeming irresponsible, uncaring, even callous or cruel, it is the priestess/medium's truth, her vision revealing that all of life, all of nature is greater than the sum of its parts.

Too much fragmentation—whether material or spiritual—means that there is no one in charge, no-one willing or able to take responsibility. Many individuals might be concerned and want to take some action— but what? This is supposedly the age where everyone is in control—we can make all the choices, decide what is right for us, 'have our say', 'email or text our opinion', 'say what we think' yet as W S Gilbert put it with such prophetic irony in *The Gondoliers:*

'When everyone is somebody,
Then no-one's anybody'.

I wrote in *Understanding Star Children:*

• *The most important thing is that we focus on our own best and highest existence, our own sense of true reality, for this is all we travellers have. We are here to work on our own imperfections, not those of others. We are here not to save the world but to save ourselves, to carry out whatever personal spiritual development may be necessary. We must never lose the sense of moving forward, of progressing.*

• *We have to exist in the material world, as inhabitants of the planet Earth. Yet unlike most other people, we are aware that at any moment we may step into another dimension. We rarely do so, but are instinctively, acutely conscious that the possibility is there.*

• *We can accept concepts that might disturb, even frighten other people—the idea, for*

292

example, that our perception of life might be nothing more than a hologram, that we have been fitted with some kind of 'microchip' which provides us with our memories and sense of reality. We do not necessarily want or need to carry out research in areas of this kind—we are likely to remain very much aware that a solid object is just that, a table is a table and not an illusion. But we can function mentally on both these levels and do not, as other people would, ask how such a thing would be possible—we know without being told how it works.

• *We do not ask why or what we are. We rarely respond on a rational, theoretical level, wanting to clarify the situation or have details spelt out. Communication between is a flowing together of mutual comprehension and understanding so that there is no need for explanations.*

• *We have access, however intuitive, to the source of all truth. Nothing further needs to be said. The rest, the acquisition of knowledge, is often only a barrier to truth, cluttering up the surface of the mirror, which should be allowed to reflect clearly what it sees without comment. In the end there are no answers, because there is no need for questions.*

- *We are seekers, rarely teachers, imparters of information or even of enlightenment. We know that once answers are given and enlightenment bestowed, there is a barrier, a boundary. An end has been reached. There is a full stop. The essence of our intuitive awareness goes far beyond such things.*

- *We do not need the consolations of an imposed doctrine—the rituals usually associated with identification of higher power, meeting with others of like minds in a common aim, asking for assistance or even carrying out familiar pleading or celebratory rites. The isolation that can prove such a heavy burden to carry becomes our greatest strength. Though part of all, we remain unique.*

Epilogue

THE GIRL WITH X-RAY EYES

I could have called this book The Girl With the X-Ray vision, or the 'X-Ray Lenses or Shades' but it goes deeper than being able to 'see' through or beyond. The focus is not on me, what I might be able to see or perceive, but on the 'Moonlit Door', the threshold itself, what it is, what it stands for, what it represents.

Everything is enclosed within a membrane of reality—we have skin, life has the boundaries of birth and death; we never manage to reach the boundaries of things like space or time, but that does not mean they are not there. If they were, they too represent further membranes of confinement, which we would call reality.

Both reality and virtual reality are meaningless in this context, because the 'Moonlit Door' is a marking point rather than a specific place. It can move, appear and disappear, it is everything and nothing. Travellers can approach it from either side, and make their enquiries. The so-called dead or the so-called living may each stand in their turn and knock, listening for the answering voices from the other side—and perhaps being equally disappointed.

The work of this medium is perhaps not to act as a channel, a way, but simply to reveal the presence of this threshold, this 'Door'. I am passive; I do not have to act, simply to be there. I used to see the role as standing at the cross-roads, wearing the cloak of the old wise woman who pointed out the various ways ahead to enquirers, helped them to see all available options.

So though the awareness is there, the ability to 'see' beyond and beneath the membrane to the core beyond, the true medium for me has been my guide Mist, who has indeed acted as a go-between and link. While at first appearing only to 'teach' or educate me in my spiritual progress, what 'he' has been doing is to allow me access to what lies beyond the membranes, beyond the many 'Moonlit Doors' that bar the way on different levels.

What lies beyond? What do I see?

I used to think it was simple clairvoyance, 'seeing clear' or 'seeing true' and it might indeed even be just that. But again, the focus is not on what I might see, it is on what is really there, and whether I see it or not is merely incidental. I have no relevance to the fact that it is there, no importance in myself.

This is the difference. The viewpoint

changes. Everything is either 'real' or 'virtually real'—life or death, even myself, the reality I seem to embody and perceive. But they are transient, irrelevant, and only the 'Moonlit Door'—the threshold—gives access to the core stability, unchanging truth and meaning beyond, which IS reality itself.

What do we call it? I don't know. Some people may call it just Truth, but that implies that everything else is a lie, and that is not so. It is something deeper, which we probably have no word for. Others may call it God, or some other name for deity, but that too is misleading because it is not a person or presence. The spirits crowding beyond the door are not a part of it, they too have their membranes of 'virtual reality' and even perceived beings like angels, archangels or gods are confined within recognizable shapes or names....

The Story Continues